✦ ✦ ✦

VANITY FAIR'S
PROUST
QUESTIONNAIRE

*101 Luminaries Ponder
Love, Death, Happiness, and the Meaning of Life*

Edited by GRAYDON CARTER

Illustrated by RISKO

RODALE

Other titles from *Vanity Fair*

———————

Vanity Fair's Tales of Hollywood
Vanity Fair, The Portraits: A Century of Iconic Images
Oscar Night: 75 Years of Hollywood Parties
Vanity Fair's Hollywood

From Robert Risko

———————

The Risko Book

✦ CONTENTS ✦

✦ CONTENTS ✦

✦ CONTENTS ✦

My most marked characteristic: "A craving to be loved, or, to be more precise, to be caressed and spoiled rather than to be admired."

—Marcel Proust, 1892

I f you are one of those for whom the very word "questionnaire" recalls the horrors of wasted afternoons
at the Department of Motor Vehicles or visits to
the emergency room or dentist's office, I have good
news in the form of a questionnaire you might find
agreeable: the list of some two dozen questions that
Marcel Proust answered in the 1880s and that, in
their modern incarnation, make up the contents of this book.

For 16 years now, *Vanity Fair* has been asking some of the
most celebrated figures of the past half-century to respond
to a set of probing personal queries as a way of taking their
psychic measure. In the process, a few misconceptions have
arisen about the enterprise (which has become a much-copied
magazine and newspaper ingredient). First, the Proust Questionnaire was dreamed up neither by *Vanity Fair* nor indeed
by Proust. It was a Parisian parlor game among the novelist's

bourgeois crowd, and it is believed to have been popularized by
the daughter of the 19th-century French president Félix Faure.

"Antoinette Faure's Album"—a red leather journal adorned
with an ornate, blind-embossed trellis—contained entries
from many in Faure's social circle. She would invite friends
over for tea and then ask each an identical sequence of questions: "[What is] your favourite virtue . . . Your idea of misery
. . . Your present state of mind?," and so forth. They would all
answer, in longhand, in her little red book.

Proust, who twice filled out Faure's form with precocious
gusto—at ages 14 and 20—subsequently published his answers as "Salon Confidences written by Marcel," in an 1892
article in *La Revue Illustrée XV.* His name would become
associated with the questionnaire posthumously (he died
of pneumonia in 1922) once Faure's list was adopted more
widely in France, Britain, and America as a form of 20th-

century pre–pop psychology. In the 1960s, in fact, *Rave,* the British music publication, made a habit of soliciting cheeky Proust responses from young rock stars. (Mick Jagger's idea of happiness at age 23? "Grovelling in weeds." And what did the Rolling Stone say he'd most like to be? "Beatle.")

As I mentioned, *Vanity Fair* took up the game in 1993. I had become editor of the magazine the previous year and sought the advice of Henry Porter (who became our London editor in 1992) about ideas for possible columns. Henry mentioned that in 1989, when he was the launch editor of London's *Sunday Correspondent* magazine, his friend Gilbert Adair, the gifted novelist (who for years had taught school in France), urged him to consider the old drawing-room diversion for the weekend magazine.

The recommendation "was greeted with widespread skepticism," Adair now recalls, "until I rather cynically pointed out that the advantage of questionnaires, from a financial point of view, was that not one of the celebrities who agree to submit [answers] expects to be paid. The suggestion was immediately adopted." The feature, Henry says, was a hit from the start "and it is one of the things that lasts from the newspaper"—in readers' Proustian memories.

I asked Henry, and Aimée Bell—an old *Spy* magazine hand who had come to *Vanity Fair* with me, and who is now one of my deputy editors—to reprise an updated version of the questionnaire in our pages, and we prepared a list of luminaries from all walks of public life who might be willing to subject themselves to the same scrutiny. We originally called the feature "Social Study," and it was conducted over the phone as an interview with *V.F.* contributor Nell Scovell,

another *Spy* veteran. Four years later, we re-christened it the "Proust Questionnaire" and soon most respondents were answering by fax and, in time, e-mail.

The page remains one of the staples of the magazine and, in looking over the entries in this book, a reader will quickly realize that the answers, whether earnest or ironic or profound, comprise 101 backstories illuminating many of the cultural giants of our age. (Indeed, in the Internet era, social-networking sites have picked up on this impulse to take quick stock of our lives through tidy lists. For a while, the Facebook questionnaire "25 Random Things About Me," for instance, became something of an obsession within a certain sector of the Bright, Young, and Self-Absorbed.)

At *Vanity Fair* we've learned a thing or two about human nature through our years of fielding Proust replies. If you're surprised by the staggering level of honesty that occasionally graces this volume (particularly among Hollywood mandarins), you're not alone. When asked to name the one thing she would change about herself, Jane Fonda responded, "My inability to have a long-term intimate relationship." When asked how she would like to die, Hedy Lamarr revealed, "Preferably after sex." (She was 85 when she gave that reply.) When asked in 2003 about his greatest extravagance, the soon-to-be governor of California, Arnold Schwarzenegger, admitted in one of the more authentically witty questionnaires we have received: "I am a major shoe queen." (His greatest fear? "I am petrified of bikini waxing. I had a very bad experience in 1978.")

When it comes to sheer effrontery, there's little doubt that comedians have been the most facile players. Martin

Short's greatest achievement: "My invention of cold fusion." The trait David Steinberg most deplores in others: "Outing a C.I.A. agent because you're pissed about something else." The phrases Elaine May most overuses: "'You're kidding' and 'Oh, fuck' and 'Oh, fuck, you're kidding.'" (Fran Lebowitz gets the prize for Best Overall Questionnaire, page 123, which she answered in comic staccato.)

On occasion, there has even been some consensus. Eight contributors said they were smitten with Paris. Two said they identified with Jesus, two with Moses, and one with *Robert* Moses (Donald Trump). The person most frequently cited as most admired? Nelson Mandela (mentioned nine times). The virtue considered most overrated? Virginity—in a landslide.

A number of people cross-referenced one another. Robert Altman named Harry Belafonte as the person he respected most; Belafonte, returning the favor, fondly recalled his appearance in Altman's film *Kansas City*. Ray Charles—Willie Nelson's "hero"—talked about his friendship with Quincy Jones, who talked about his debt to Sidney Poitier. Timothy Leary praised Yoko Ono, who, when asked to name her heroes in real life, replied, simply, "Me."

As Ono's answer implies, virtually everyone had at least one or two moments of pure, unbridled candor. What would Karl Rove change? "[I'd] be more patient." (I'll say.) Ted Kennedy? "I'd have won in 1980." And several, naturally, admitted that death was their darkest fear. "Trust me," insisted Larry King, who survived a heart attack in 1987. "I saw no lights, no angels—nothing." (You may also notice that a number of individuals herein are no longer among us: Altman, Leary, Claudette Colbert, and Norman Mailer all died shortly after their questionnaires were published.)

Amid the tumult and the dread, amid these many attempts to tackle the overarching issues of love and death and the meaning of life, there are flashes of Proustian poetry. Allen Ginsberg's most marked characteristic, he said, was his "incriminating eloquence." While Julia Child most abhorred "a dreadful meal badly served," William F. Buckley Jr. claimed to hate "lousy logic, tempestuously waged." Joan Didion, when asked "When were you happiest?," referred to a character in a passage from her novel *Democracy:* "She recalled being extremely happy eating lunch by herself in a hotel room in Chicago, once when snow was drifting on the window ledges." And Johnny Cash offered this six-word description of paradise: "This morning, with her, having coffee." (You can try your own hand at playing Proust. Invite a few friends over, flip to the back of this book—we've provided a blank questionnaire—and just pass around the quill pen and the madeleines.)

Finally, you'll see that each set of responses in this volume is accompanied by an illustration from the fertile mind and impeccable brush of Robert Risko. In terms of celebrity caricature, no one is better at compressing the essence of a single subject into a few exuberant lines. Risko's genius at compression, in fact, conjures up the Jazz Age *Vanity Fair,* which, between the wars, featured the drawings of similarly bold stylists, such as Miguel Covarrubias, Will Cotton, and Paolo Garretto. It is this economy of expression that makes Risko's drawings a perfect complement to the succinct queries that Faure and Proust perfected at the dawn of the Belle Époque, 120 years ago.

GRAYDON CARTER
New York City, 2009

ROBERT ALTMAN

FILMMAKER

My greatest regret: "Doing this questionnaire."

What is your idea of perfect happiness?
Screening a new picture in a room full of "virgins."

What is your greatest fear?
See above answer.

Which historical figure do you most identify with?
Buffalo Bill.

Which living person do you most admire?
Harry Belafonte.

What is the trait you most deplore in yourself?
My tendency to take foolish risks.

What is the trait you most deplore in others?
Their reluctance to take foolish risks.

What do you consider the most overrated virtue?
Frugality.

On what occasion do you lie?
What day is today?

Which living person do you most despise?
W.

Which words or phrases do you most overuse?
"Cut."

What is your greatest regret?
Doing this questionnaire.

What or who is the greatest love of your life?
Kathryn Reed.

When and where were you happiest?
Working.

Which talent would you most like to have?
Card counting.

What is your current state of mind?
Cautiously optimistic.

If you could change one thing about yourself, what would it be?
I'd make my legs the same length.

If you could change one thing about your family, what would it be?
No comment.

What do you consider your greatest achievement?
I've made only the movies I wanted to make.

If you were to die and come back as a person or thing, what do you think it would be?
I'm immortal.

What is your most treasured possession?
Memories.

What is the quality you most like in a man?
The ability not to take one's self seriously.

What is the quality you most like in a woman?
The ability to take *me* seriously.

Who are your favorite writers?
Raymond Carver and Roald Dahl.

Who is your favorite hero of fiction?
Philip Marlowe.

What is it that you most dislike?
Movies that explain everything.

What is your motto?
"Giggle and give in."

April 2006
(Altman died in November 2006.)

JULIE ANDREWS

ACTRESS

What is your idea of perfect happiness?
Can I get back to you on that?

What is your greatest fear?
Fear!

What is your most marked characteristic?
I bet you thought I was going to say my nose.

What is the trait you most deplore in yourself?
I interrupt too much.

Which living person do you most despise?
'enry 'iggins!

What is your greatest extravagance?
Flowers.

What is your current state of mind?
Hopeful.

What do you consider the most overrated virtue?
Chastity.

On what occasion do you lie?
Occasionally. If I feel it's kinder than the truth.

What do you dislike most about your appearance?
My nose.

What is the quality you most like in a man?
Intelligence and a sense of humor.

What is the quality you most like in a woman?
A sense of humor and intelligence.

Which words or phrases do you most overuse?
"Do you know what I mean?" or "Are you all right?"

What or who is the greatest love of your life?
My family.

When and where were you happiest?
In London. When Blake [Edwards, her husband since 1969] made me laugh so much I wept. Blake says I slept with a smile.

If you could change one thing about yourself, what would it be?
My nose.

Which talent would you most like to have?
Next time around, I plan to be a classical composer.

What do you consider your greatest achievement?
The miracle of giving birth.

If you were to die and come back as a person or thing, what do you think it would be?
A meadowlark.

Where would you like to live?
Where there are meadowlarks.

What is your most treasured possession?
Family photographs.

What do you regard as the lowest depth of misery?
Being without hope.

What is your favorite occupation?
Pottering in my garden.

Who is your favorite hero of fiction?
Charlie Brown.

What are your favorite names?
Those of my children, grandchildren, and great-grandchildren.

What is it that you most dislike?
Poverty, hunger, unhappiness.

How would you like to die?
Peacefully—holding my mate.

What is your motto?
"When in doubt, stand still."

April 2008

"Next time around, I plan to be a classical composer."

"Sometimes I'd like to take a break from being the *padrino.*"

What is your current state of mind?
Serene, after my first 60 years.

Which historical figure do you most identify with?
Achilles—the fierce warrior.

What do you consider your greatest achievement?
That my work is also my fun.

What is your greatest extravagance?
Insatiable perfectionism.

What is your favorite journey?
The ones I take in my head.

What is your greatest fear?
Losing my health and well-being.

Which living person do you most admire?
Any Nobel Prize winner.

Which living person do you most despise?
All vulgar people.

What is the trait you most deplore in others?
Disloyalty.

On what occasion do you lie?
Like all sincere people, when I absolutely can't avoid it.

What is your greatest regret?
That I didn't start working when I was 20. That way, I'd have more time left to be "Giorgio Armani."

Which words or phrases do you most overuse?
"*Disgraziato!*"

If you could change one thing about yourself, what would it be?
I wish I was a little more naïve.

What do you dislike most about your appearance?
Help! I'm missing at least five inches in height.

What is the quality you most like in a man?
When he knows the right moment to speak, and the right moment to shut up.

What is the quality you most like in a woman?
When she doesn't think she already knows all the secrets.

What or who is the greatest love of your life?
The current one.

What is your most treasured possession?
Love requited.

If you could change one thing about your family, what would it be?
Like all Italians, I adore my family, but sometimes I'd like to take a break from being the "*padrino.*"

What do you most value in your friends?
Availability and discretion.

If you were to die and come back as a person or thing, what do you think it would be?
As a libertine—the opposite of what I am.

If you could choose what to come back as, what would it be?
As a cat, lazy and aloof.

How would you like to die?
Knowing I've left a positive mark.

What is your motto?
"Advance, but cherish your past."

May 1995

GIORGIO ARMANI

FASHION DESIGNER

Perfect happiness: "A canoe, mixed sun and cloud, no deadlines in sight."

What is your idea of perfect happiness?
A canoe, mixed sun and cloud, no deadlines in sight.

What is your greatest fear?
A bear attack in a forest fire.

Which living person do you most admire?
Anonymous. She's working to make the planet greener.

What is the trait you most deplore in others?
Ineffectual whining.

What is your greatest extravagance?
Mad, gamble-packed entrepreneurial enterprises, such as writing.

What is your favorite journey?
The Ottawa River by boat. Although I've never done it.

On what occasion do you lie?
When asked about other people's clothing choices.

Which living person do you most despise?
Major polluters.

Which words or phrases do you most overuse?
"If I were you I would . . . " "Maybe it's for the best." "Never mind."

What is your greatest regret?
Not being an opera singer.

When and where were you happiest?
At 7:59 P.M. on May 17, 1976, in Toronto. That's the Exact Minute our daughter was born. Soppy answer, but true.

What is your current state of mind?
Lazy, anxious, and distracted. But I've learned to live with it.

If you could change one thing about yourself, what would it be?
I'd stop saying yes to inessential requests.

What do you consider your greatest achievement?
"Greatest" is too big a word. The most thrilling one for me was my first professional publication, at age 20.

If you were to die and come back as a person or thing, what do you think it would be?
A snail.

If you could choose what to come back as, what would it be?
A raven.

What is your most treasured possession?
That stone cat on my front porch. Give it back, whoever took it!

What do you regard as the lowest depth of misery?
No good news.

Where would you like to live?
In a tree.

What is your favorite occupation?
Sleeping. That way you don't have to deal with "No good news."

What is your most marked characteristic?
Unjustifiable optimism.

What is the quality you most like in a man?
Funny, smart, unjustifiably optimistic, and good at taking the lids off jars.

What is the quality you most like in a woman?
Funny, smart, unjustifiably optimistic, and a superlative gossip.

What is it that you most dislike?
Politicians who lie about important things other than clothing choices, and use those lies for exploitation, power grabs, global-warming evasion, and personal profit.

How would you like to die?
Of a painless disease, with a month's warning, on a spring day, with some good news in hand.

What is your motto?
"Nolite te bastardes carborundorum."
[Don't let the bastards grind you down.]

October 2006

MARGARET ATWOOD

WRITER

LAUREN BACALL

ACTRESS

The most overrated virtue: "A 24-inch waist."

What is your idea of perfect happiness?
Waking up in the morning.

What is your greatest fear?
Not waking up in the morning.

Which historical figure do you most identify with?
Marie Antoinette.

Which living person do you most admire?
No one I can think of offhand.

What is the trait you most deplore in yourself?
Thinking.

What is the trait you most deplore in others?
Not thinking.

What is your greatest extravagance?
Spending.

What is your favorite journey?
Paris.

What do you consider the most overrated virtue?
A 24-inch waist.

On what occasion do you lie?
Only when I'm sure I'm not going to get caught.

If you were to die and come back as a person or thing, what do you think it would be?
Fred Astaire.

What is your most treasured possession?
My feet.

What do you regard as the lowest depth of misery?
Continual unemployment.

Where would you like to live?
Anywhere but here.

What is your favorite occupation?
Beefing.

What is your most marked characteristic?
Beefing.

What is the quality you most like in a man?
Humor.

What is the quality you most like in a woman?
Humor.

What do you most value in your friends?
Humor.

Who are your favorite writers?
Tennessee Williams.

Who is your favorite hero of fiction?
The Scarlet Pimpernel.

Who are your heroes in real life?
My sons.

What are your favorite names?
Stephen, Leslie, Sam, Sophie.

What is it that you most dislike?
My face.

How would you like to die?
I would not like it.

What is your motto?
"Do not what I would do unless I tell you to."

April 2004

BRIGITTE BARDOT

ACTRESS *and* ANIMAL-RIGHTS ACTIVIST

What or who is the greatest love of your life?
Animals, animals, animals, animals . . .

Which living person do you most admire?
None.

What is your greatest extravagance?
My love for animals!

If you could change one thing about yourself, what would it be?
Nothing about me. Everything about others.

What is your greatest regret?
Not being a fairy!

What is your favorite journey?
The one in my craziest dreams.

What do you most value in your friends?
Their faithfulness. The fact that after all these years they are still my friends. I have very few friends.

What is your idea of perfect happiness?
Perfect happiness does not exist. But happily there are not always awful misfortunes.

When and where were you happiest?
Never, but I am still waiting!

Which talent would you most like to have?
To make miracles.

What do you consider the most overrated virtue?
Social status.

What do you consider your greatest achievement?
My foundation for the protection of animals, created in 1986 and officially recognized in 1991.

What is your most marked characteristic?
My courage.

Which living person do you most despise?
Hunters!

What is your most treasured possession?
My animals. Everything that can't be bought with money.

What are your favorite occupations?
Taking care of animals, reading, doing crosswords, and cooking vegetarian food—cakes!

What do you dislike most about your appearance?
At the moment, I'm giving a wholesale price on the entire package as an end-of-season sale.

On what occasion do you lie?
Never!

Which historical figure do you most identify with?
Saint Francis of Assisi.

Who is your favorite hero of fiction?
Don Quixote, because I am like him in my struggle.

Who are your heroes in real life?
Joan of Arc, King Louis XVI, Dian Fossey, and Professor Claude Reiss, who is fighting against vivisection.

If you were to die and come back as a person or thing, what do you think it would be?
I have no desire to be reincarnated, as a thing or a person. This life's enough for me!!

How would you like to die?
Gently.

What is your motto?
"Noise does no good, goodness doesn't make noise."

December 1994

My greatest love: "Animals, animals, animals, animals . . ."

My greatest regret: "Not being a banana."

Which words or phrases do you most overuse?
"Day-O."

What is your greatest regret?
Not being a banana.

What is your idea of perfect happiness?
A world without violence or poverty.

What is your greatest fear?
The Republicans will win everything.

What is it that you most dislike?
Racism.

Which historical figure do you most identify with?
Paul Robeson.

Which living person do you most admire?
Nelson Mandela.

Which living person do you most despise?
Clarence Thomas.

Which talent would you most like to have?
To compose like Duke Ellington and to sing like Odetta.

What is your most treasured possession?
A good song.

Where would you like to live?
In Carnegie Hall.

What is the trait you most deplore in yourself?
My self-doubt.

What is the trait you most deplore in others?
Blindly following.

What is your greatest extravagance?
Watching CNN.

What is your favorite journey?
Looking for leaders.

When and where were you happiest?
Playing Seldom Seen in Bob Altman's film *Kansas City*.

What is your most marked characteristic?
Bluntness.

What is the quality you most like in a man?
His constant state of trying to discover.

What is the quality you most like in a woman?
Being a liberated woman.

What or who is the greatest love of your life?
My family.

If you were to die and come back as a person or thing, what do you think it would be?
A guitar.

If you could choose what to come back as, what would it be?
Something we've never heard of.

How would you like to die?
Slowly, over a 200-year period, without pain.

What is your motto?
"LIVE!"

September 1995

HARRY BELAFONTE

ENTERTAINER *and* CIVIL-RIGHTS ACTIVIST

ANNETTE BENING

ACTRESS

My greatest extravagance: "Massages, expensive lingerie, and lots of shoes."

What is your idea of perfect happiness?
Solitude.

What is your greatest fear?
Losing my mind.

Which historical figure do you most identify with?
Victoria Woodhull, the turn-of-the-century presidential candidate, feminist, and advocate of free love.

What is the trait you most deplore in yourself?
Harsh self-criticism.

What is your greatest extravagance?
Massages, expensive lingerie, and lots of shoes.

What do you consider the most overrated virtue?
Virginity.

Which words or phrases do you most overuse?
"You know" and "Fuck it."

What or who is the greatest love of your life?
I am married to him.

When and where were you happiest?
First, conceiving, and second, giving birth.

What is your current state of mind?
Confused, amused, and curious.

If you could change one thing about yourself, what would it be?
My need to rush.

What do you consider your greatest achievement?
Driving across town with a thirsty five-year-old, a pissed-off two-and-a-half-year-old, and a hungry newborn.

What is the quality you most like in a man?
Passion.

What is the quality you most like in a woman?
Wit.

Who are your favorite writers?
Shakespeare; Chekhov; George Bernard Shaw; Thornton Wilder; Maureen Dowd, columnist; Germaine Greer, especially her latest book, *The Whole Woman*. It's infuriating, funny, and provocative.

Who is your favorite hero of fiction?
Nora from Ibsen's *A Doll's House*.

Who are your heroes in real life?
Eva Le Gallienne, Ruth Gordon, Maggie Smith, Daniel Moynihan, Václav Havel, B. K. S. Iyengar, and Ann Roth (costume designer for five decades, who won the Academy Award for *The English Patient*). She [Roth] has boundless energy, great taste, and infectious joy. I want to be her when I grow up.

What are your favorite names?
Kathlyn, Benjamin, Isabel.

What is it that you most dislike?
Root beer.

How would you like to die?
Quickly and painlessly at a very old age, napping on my porch swing.

November 1999

TONY BENNETT

ENTERTAINER

"You're only as good as your next performance."

What is your favorite occupation?
Being an entertainer.

What or who is the greatest love of your life?
Me.

When and where were you happiest?
Right now!

What is your greatest regret?
I could have been a contender.

What is your idea of perfect happiness?
A loving life.

Which historical figure do you most identify with?
Jesus.

Which living person do you most admire?
Former New York governor Mario Cuomo.

What is your greatest extravagance?
My Visa card.

What is your favorite journey?
To Rio.

What do you consider the most overrated virtue?
No virtue is overrated—I respect all of them.

Which living person do you most despise?
My personal tax collector.

Which words or phrases do you most overuse?
"Yes," "straight ahead," and "if you know what I mean."

What is your current state of mind?
Mellow.

If you could change one thing about yourself, what would it be?
To achieve more discipline.

If you could change one thing about your family, what would it be?
Tell them to stop moving out of town.

Where would you like to live?
N.Y.C. (the Apple).

What is your most marked characteristic?
Searching.

What do you most value in your friends?
Love.

Who is your favorite hero of fiction?
Sherlock Holmes.

What are your favorite names?
Gandhi, Martin Luther King, Mandela.

What is it that you most dislike?
Bigotry.

How would you like to die?
In my sleep, having a lovely dream.

If you could choose what to come back as, what would it be?
A butterfly.

What is your motto?
"You're only as good as your next performance."

December 1998

My motto: "Kiss 'em, slap 'em, send 'em home."

What is your idea of perfect happiness?
A cross-country road trip with a new lover and my baby riding shotgun.

Which historical figure do you most identify with?
I can tell you what historical figure is most associated with me: Sarah Bernhardt. Unfortunately she's not here to comment.

What is your greatest extravagance?
My open account with a high-class escort service and a standing reservation at the Carlyle.

What is your favorite journey?
Steve Perry.

On what occasion do you lie?
Onstage, during interviews, during grand-jury testimony, when I get pulled over for speeding, and when I come through customs after a shopping extravaganza in a Third World country.

Which living person do you most despise?
The stinky taxi driver who picked me up at 14th and Eighth on December 1, 1998, at approximately 5:15 P.M.

What is your greatest regret?
A recent tension-fraught lunch with a supermodel.

When and where were you happiest?
The weeklong anticipation before a recent tension-fraught lunch with a supermodel (which I now regret).

Which talent would you most like to have?
The ability to bullshit my way into a major motion picture.

What is your current state of mind?
Whacked out on muscle relaxants and echinacea.

What is your most treasured possession?
My mucus plug—it sits on my desk in a snow globe.

Where would you like to live?
1006 Bluff Ridge Drive, New Albany, Indiana.

What is your most marked characteristic?
A tiny mole on the bottom of my foot.

What is the quality you most like in a man?
Lots of prickly ear hair.

What is the quality you most like in a woman?
A shrill, bitchy edge that never stops.

Who is your favorite hero of fiction?
Neely O'Hara.

What are your favorite names?
Ezekiel, Tina, Mickey, Tilly, Loulou, Maurice, Herminio.

What is it that you most dislike?
Bottom-feeders.

What is your motto?
"Kiss 'em, slap 'em, send 'em home."

August 1999

SANDRA BERNHARD

COMEDIAN

BILL BLASS

FASHION DESIGNER

The occasion on which I lie: "When in love."

What do you consider your greatest achievement?
Surviving in a business as volatile as fashion.

What is your greatest fear?
The next collection.

What is your current state of mind?
Up.

Which words or phrases do you most overuse?
"Chic."

Which living person do you most admire?
You, dear reader.

Which historical figure do you most identify with?
Thomas Jefferson.

What is your greatest extravagance?
Collecting furniture and pictures. Objects.

What is your most treasured possession?
The last thing I bought.

When and where were you happiest?
Any summer day in the country.

What do you consider the most overrated virtue?
Ambition resulting in celebrity.

What is the trait you most deplore in yourself?
Lethargy. Indolence.

What is the trait you most deplore in others?
Bad manners.

On what occasion do you lie?
When in love.

What or who is the greatest love of your life?
My dogs.

What are your favorite names?
Barnaby, Sebastian.

What do you dislike most about your appearance?
The 40 pounds *not* disappearing.

Which talent would you most like to have?
To be able to tango.

What do you regard as the lowest depth of misery?
Illness.

What is your favorite occupation?
Bullfighting.

What is your most marked characteristic?
Curiosity.

What is the quality you most like in a man?
Honesty and bravery.

What is the quality you most like in a woman?
Complete honesty and lack of bravery.

What do you most value in your friends?
Space.

Who are your favorite writers?
Thackeray, Cather, Cormac McCarthy.

What is it that you most dislike?
Late nights, late dinners, late appointments.

If you were to die and could choose what to come back as, what would it be?
An oak tree.

What is your motto?
"A stitch in time . . . "

August 1995
(Blass died in 2002.)

DAVID BOWIE

MUSICIAN

My greatest fear: "Converting kilometers to miles."

What is your idea of perfect happiness?
Reading.

What is your most marked characteristic?
Getting a word in edgewise.

What do you consider your greatest achievement?
Discovering morning.

What is your greatest fear?
Converting kilometers to miles.

Which historical figure do you most identify with?
Santa Claus.

Which living person do you most admire?
Elvis.

Who are your heroes in real life?
The consumer.

What is the trait you most deplore in yourself?
While in New York, tolerance.
Outside of New York, intolerance.

What is the trait you most deplore in others?
Talent.

What is your favorite journey?
The road of artistic excess.

What do you consider the most overrated virtue?
Sympathy and originality.

Which words or phrases do you most overuse?
"Chthonic," "miasma."

What is your greatest regret?
That I never wore bell-bottoms.

What is your current state of mind?
Pregnant.

If you could change one thing about your family, what would it be?
My fear of them (wife and son excluded).

What is your most treasured possession?
A photograph held together by cellophane tape of Little Richard that I bought in 1958, and a pressed and dried chrysanthemum picked on my honeymoon in Kyoto.

What do you regard as the lowest depth of misery?
Living in fear.

Where would you like to live?
Northeast Bali or south Java.

What is your favorite occupation?
Squishing paint about a senseless canvas.

What is the quality you most like in a man?
The ability to return books.

What is the quality you most like in a woman?
The ability to burp on command.

What are your favorite names?
Sears & Roebuck.

What is your motto?
"What" *is* my motto.

August 1998

JAMES BROWN

MUSICIAN

"Integrity…takes care of everything."

What is your idea of perfect happiness?
Being able to work a lot and play a little bit.

What is your greatest fear?
That we won't be able to get the kids schooled in time, and that we will probably lose two or three generations—unless they go with positive music and all the positive avenues.

Which historical figure do you most identify with?
Geronimo.

Which living person do you most admire?
I've never met the man, but Nelson Mandela. The man spent 27 years in prison, came out, became president, and won what he fought for.

What is the trait you most deplore in others?
I would never say anything; that's God's job.

What is your greatest regret?
That I don't know more about American Indians.

What is your greatest extravagance?
I'd have to say watches and cars. It would be music if it wasn't my profession.

When and where were you happiest?
When I got "Please, Please, Please" out and shoes on my feet.

Which talent would you most like to have?
You know, that would be greedy. God gave me enough talent to accelerate to where I'm at. I don't want any more than I've got.

What do you consider your greatest achievement?
Going to church and belonging to a faith, which is the Baptist Church.

What do you regard as the lowest depth of misery?
I consider the worst times of my life to be when I was locked up—when you lose a complete day and you don't accomplish anything.

What is the quality you most like in a man?
Integrity—that takes care of everything. Take care of your kids, watch your family, try to be a good man, walk as close as you can to what you believe in.

What do you most value in your friends?
Undying determination; long-lasting loyalty, if I can get it.

What are your favorite names?
My name—a biblical name, James Joseph. And for a woman's name, Mary.

What is it that you most dislike?
Laziness.

How would you like to die?
I wouldn't.

What is your motto?
"Live as long as you can and die when you can't help it."

November 2002
(Brown died in 2006.)

What is your idea of perfect happiness?
All commitments fulfilled.

What is your greatest fear?
War.

Which historical figure do you most identify with?
Jesus.

What is the trait you most deplore in yourself?
Inadequacy.

What is the trait you most deplore in others?
Procrastination.

What do you consider the most overrated virtue?
Self-confidence, when it morphs into a know-it-all attitude.

On what occasion do you lie?
To avoid hurting someone, or when I forget the truth.

What do you dislike most about your appearance?
My nose.

Which words or phrases do you most overuse?
"Write that down" or "groovy."

What is your greatest regret?
That more people have not heard my composition "Regret," recorded by the London Symphony.

What or who is the greatest love of your life?
The what is music, the who are my wife and family.

When and where were you happiest?
May 8, 1945, Regensburg, Germany, the end of World War II in Europe.

If you could change one thing about yourself, what would it be?
A more retentive mind.

If you could change one thing about your family, what would it be?
For each to be fulfilled.

If you were to die and come back as a person or thing, what do you think it would be?
A piano.

If you could choose what to come back as, what would it be?
Johann Sebastian Bach.

What is your most treasured possession?
Faith.

What do you regard as the lowest depth of misery?
Betrayal.

What is it that you most dislike?
The suffering of innocents.

Who are your favorite writers?
Dostoyevsky, Thomas Mann, and Mark Twain.

Who is your favorite hero of fiction?
Huckleberry Finn.

Who are your heroes in real life?
John Paul II, Martin Luther King Jr., Rosa Parks, and Darius Milhaud.

What are your favorite names?
The names we gave our children: Darius (after Darius Milhaud), Michael, Christopher, Catherine, Daniel, and Matthew.

How would you like to die?
Playing stride piano.

What is your motto?
"Hang in and hang on."

March 2006

I was happiest: "May 8, 1945, Germany, the end of World War II in Europe."

DAVE BRUBECK

JAZZ PIANIST *and* COMPOSER

"I'd like to know how to pray better."

What is your idea of perfect happiness?
Heaven.

What is your greatest fear?
Hell.

What is the trait you most deplore in yourself?
My failure to practice the harpsichord more regularly.

What is the trait you most deplore in others?
Their failure to ask me to play the harpsichord.

What is your greatest extravagance?
My lifestyle.

What is your favorite journey?
Going home.

What do you consider the most overrated virtue?
Introspection.

On what occasion do you lie?
On many occasions.

What do you dislike most about your appearance?
My gestating paunch.

Which words or phrases do you most overuse?
"In due course … "

What is your greatest regret?
I read slowly.

What or who is the greatest love of your life?
J. S. Bach.

When and where were you happiest?
Ages five to seven.

Which talent would you most like to have?
A retentive and comprehensive memory.

What is your current state of mind?
Apprehensive.

If you could change one thing about yourself, what would it be?
I'd like to know how to pray better.

If you could change one thing about your family, what would it be?
I'd like it to be larger.

What do you consider your greatest achievement?
National Review.

If you could choose how to come back, how would it be?
Stillborn.

What is your most treasured possession?
My faith.

What do you regard as the lowest depth of misery?
The loss of faith.

Where would you like to live?
Where I live.

What is your favorite occupation?
The correction of other people's errors.

What is your most marked characteristic?
Speedwriting.

What is the quality you most like in a person?
A sense of humor.

What do you most value in your friends?
Their companionship.

Who are your favorite writers?
Wilfrid Sheed, John Leonard, Richard Brookhiser, Joe Sobran, D. Keith Mano, Murray Kempton.

Who is your favorite hero of fiction?
Blackford Oakes.

Who are your heroes in real life?
The people who overthrew the Soviet Union.

What is it that you most dislike?
Lousy logic, tempestuously waged.

How would you like to die?
Painlessly.

What is your motto?
"Quod licet Jovi, non licet bovi."
[What is permitted to Jove is not permitted to swine (ox).]

September 1993
(Buckley died in 2008.)

WILLIAM F. BUCKLEY JR.

WRITER *and* EDITOR

JIMMY BUFFETT

MUSICIAN

My favorite journey: "Paris, always Paris."

What is your most treasured possession?
My first Martin guitar.

What is your idea of perfect happiness?
Having my own island.

Where would you like to live?
Where I do.

When and where were you happiest?
I still am.

What is your current state of mind?
Still crazy after all these years. (I wish I had written that song.)

What is your most marked characteristic?
My sense of humor.

What is your favorite occupation?
Flying.

What is your greatest extravagance?
Airplanes.

What is your greatest fear?
Earthquakes.

Which historical figure do you most identify with?
Jean Laffite, the pirate.

Which living person do you most admire?
Walter Cronkite.

What do you consider the most overrated virtue?
Chastity.

What is the trait you most deplore in others?
Greed.

What is your favorite journey?
Paris, always Paris.

What do you dislike most about your appearance?
Somebody stole my hair.

Which words or phrases do you most overuse?
Curse words.

What is your greatest regret?
That I never taped or documented my grandfather's stories of his years at sea.

What or who is the greatest love of your life?
I really love my life.

Who are your favorite writers?
Mark Twain, Eudora Welty, and Patrick O'Brian.

How would you like to die?
Quietly on an island.

If you were to die and come back as a person or thing, what do you think it would be?
Osprey.

What is your motto?
"Never forget to duck."

June 1998

SIR MICHAEL CAINE

ACTOR

What is your idea of perfect happiness?
Being at home, in England. I have a house in the country there, and that's where I'm always happiest.

What is your greatest fear?
As I was born very poor, I suppose going back to poverty again.

Which historical figure do you most identify with?
Cary Grant. I like Cary Grant. And I knew him. He was a friend of mine. But now he's dead, so he's a historical figure, especially in the cinema industry.

Which living person do you most admire?
I think it has to be President Mandela.

What is your current state of mind?
I'm amazed that I'm still here in this business, as happy as I am.

What is the trait you most deplore in yourself?
I very rarely lose my temper, but it's not very pretty, and I always regret it. I avoid it at all costs.

What do you dislike most about your appearance?
At the moment, it's my haircut. You know, when you're an actor, you have to have hair for the next part. And I'm playing an old grandfather, and I always wear short hair, and my hair is the longest it's been for 10 years.

Which living person do you most despise?
I have a rule of keeping all negatives out of my life, so if there was someone I was going to despise, I wouldn't waste the energy on them—they disappear. I remember a philosopher said to me once, "You should only hate people you love. The rest of them are not worth the energy."

Which words or phrases do you most overuse?
I'm always saying "You know what I mean?" to people, because where I grew up a lot of people never knew what I meant.

What is your greatest regret?
My father died when I was sort of a down-and-out actor, completely desolate. He never saw any of my success.

What or who is the greatest love of your life?
That's easy: my wife, Shakira.

Which talent would you most like to have?
Tap dancing. I love tap dancing. I think it's great.

If you could change one thing about your family, what would it be?
My parents would be alive.

If you were to die and come back as a person or thing, what do you think it would be?
I'd come back as me. I've had the best possible life. I can't think of anyone else I'd rather be.

If you could choose what to come back as, what would it be?
A turtle. I'd like to slow down and live a lot longer.

What do you regard as the lowest depth of misery?
Being a soldier in a war, which I've been.

Who are your favorite writers?
Probably Raymond Chandler and James Ellroy. I like thrillers. I'm one of those kinds of guys. And the latest one, Michael Connelly.

What are your favorite names?
Well, my real name is Maurice, so Michael for men, 'cause I chose it myself. And my daughters' names are Dominique and Natasha. Dominique is the heroine of Ayn Rand's *The Fountainhead,* and Natasha is my favorite other name.

How would you like to die?
Later and asleep.

What is your motto?
"No good turn goes unpunished."

February 2004

"No good turn goes unpunished."

GEORGE CARLIN

COMEDIAN

My motto: "Always have a good motto."

What is your greatest fear?
To lose the power of speech.

Which historical figure do you most identify with?
No one so far.

Which living person do you most admire?
I don't spend a lot of time admiring people.

What is the trait you most deplore in yourself?
My inability to relax and do nothing.

What do you consider the most overrated virtue?
Courage.

On what occasion do you lie?
To protect people's feelings.

What do you dislike most about your appearance?
My left arm is 13 inches shorter than my right.

What is your greatest regret?
Having wasted nine perfectly good years in school.

What or who is the greatest love of your life?
Sally Wade, the Pearl of the Ozarks.

When and where were you happiest?
Home alone after school, before my mother got home from work.

Which talent would you most like to have?
To be able to play great boogie-woogie piano.

What do you consider your greatest achievement?
Sustaining in my field and improving over time.

What is your most marked characteristic?
Positive attitude.

What is the quality you most like in a man?
Honesty.

What is the quality you most like in a woman?
Toughness.

What do you most value in your friends?
Their ability to exchange overcoats while running at full speed.

What is your most treasured possession?
Charlie Parker's autograph. I got it at Birdland when I was 15. And a medal: Best Entertainer, 1949, Camp Notre Dame. I still wear it.

What do you regard as the lowest depth of misery?
To be cold, sick, broke, hungry, lonely, forgotten, and dying.

Where would you like to live?
I guess right there at home would be a pretty good place.

Who is your favorite hero of fiction?
I'm not interested in make-believe people.

Who are your heroes in real life?
No one should have heroes. It is degrading.

What are your favorite names?
Fortescu Dalrymple, Tinky Pringle, and Sympathetic Hah.

What is it that you most dislike?
Organized religion.

How would you like to die?
To just explode spontaneously in someone's living room.

What is your motto?
"Always have a good motto."

May 2001
(Carlin died in 2008.)

My favorite journey: "The last mile home."

What is your favorite occupation?
Performing.

What is your greatest fear?
Losing my voice in concert.

What is your idea of perfect happiness?
Home from a tour . . . walking barefoot in my house and yard.

What do you regard as the lowest depth of misery?
A week on amphetamines, and coming down.

What is your most marked characteristic?
The scar on my face.

What do you dislike most about your appearance?
My beat-up, cut-up face.

What is your greatest extravagance?
Giving money.

What is the trait you most deplore in yourself?
My inability to remember the names of important people I meet.

What is the trait you most deplore in others?
Gossip.

What is your favorite journey?
The last mile home.

What do you consider the most overrated virtue?
Legend.

On what occasion do you lie?
I don't know; try to catch me.

Which words or phrases do you most overuse?
"Great!," "Good."

Which living person do you most despise?
Fathers who won't pay child support.

What or who is the greatest love of your life?
June Carter.

When and where were you happiest?
This morning, with her, having coffee.

Which talent would you most like to have?
A perfect-pitch voice.

What do you consider your greatest achievement?
Being inducted into the Country Music Hall of Fame.

What is your greatest regret?
That I couldn't go to college.

What is your most treasured possession?
My mother's Bible.

What is the quality you most like in a man?
Humility.

What is the quality you most like in a woman?
Beauty inside and out.

Who are your heroes in real life?
My son, John Carter Cash, and Evander Holyfield.

How would you like to die?
Onstage or in my sleep.

If you were to die and come back as a person or thing, what do you think it would be?
Dust on the wind.

If you could choose what to come back as, what would it be?
A tree like the one Joyce Kilmer wrote the poem about.

What is your motto?
"Better times will come" is the ancient Cash-family motto. Better times came for me.

November 1997
(Cash died in 2003.)

JOHNNY CASH

MUSICIAN

RAY CHARLES

MUSICIAN

"God helps those who help themselves."

What is your idea of perfect happiness?
A great performance when everything comes together: the music, the audience—the whole thing. It's what makes me want to keep touring and recording.

Which historical figure do you most identify with?
Martin Luther King Jr. He was a man who made a difference and stood for something in life. He had guts, and a lot of people have benefited from his courage.

What is the trait you most deplore in yourself?
My inability to slow down.

What do you consider the most overrated virtue?
Talent. People with very little of it are packaged and marketed like crazy these days, especially in music. The true talents are few and far between. Original talent is especially lacking. Everything and everyone sounds the same.

Which talent would you most like to have?
That's a tough one. Maybe be the world chess champion. I love that game. The pros tell me I'm pretty good!

If you were to die and come back as a person or thing, what do you think it would be?
That's a wild question. I'd probably come back as an instrument—that's how much I love music.

What is your most treasured possession?
My hands. They guide everywhere I go, and they allow me to play the piano and other instruments, which has been my lifeline since an early age.

What do you regard as the lowest depth of misery?
Racism and poverty. Two scourges that I have known since early in my life. Sadly, while things are better for many, there are those who still suffer the indignities of both. Until we find a way to fix these problems, there will always be unrest in our society and our world.

What do you most value in your friends?
Loyalty. Many of them date back many years. Quincy Jones and I met at the beginning of our careers, never knowing they would be so full and long-lasting. Over the years, we've helped each other out.

Who are your heroes in real life?
The everyday people who get up and go to work, feed their kids, and try to do the right thing. They're my real heroes. They're the people who come and see my shows, spend their hard-earned money, and I appreciate their loyalty and support.

How would you like to die?
Peacefully, when the good Lord is ready to call my number.

What is your motto?
"God helps those who help themselves."

February 2003
(Charles died in 2004.)

JULIA CHILD

CHEF *and* AUTHOR

What is your idea of perfect happiness?
A great meal with dear friends.

What do you regard as the lowest depth of misery?
A dreadful meal badly served.

What do you consider your greatest achievement?
The making of French bread—back in the 1970s.

What is your favorite occupation?
My work.

What is your greatest fear?
Having gastro difficulties.

Which historical figure do you most identify with?
Escoffier.

Where would you like to live?
In Santa Barbara and Cambridge.

What is your favorite journey?
To Paris.

When and where were you happiest?
In Paris—the 1950s.

What or who is the greatest love of your life?
My late husband.

Which living person do you most admire?
Hillary Clinton.

What is your greatest extravagance?
Shoes.

What is the quality you most like in a man?
A big, strong, jolly man who loves his work, and me.

What is the quality you most like in a woman?
Fun and interesting to be with.

What is the trait you most deplore in yourself?
Forgetting names.

What is the trait you most deplore in others?
Being an extremist of any sort.

Which living person do you most despise?
An extremist of any kind.

What is it that you most dislike?
Rigid, uncompromising, angry extremists.

What do you consider the most overrated virtue?
Holiness.

If you could change one thing about yourself, what would it be?
Easier hair.

If you could change one thing about your family, what would it be?
To have them all very healthy and 25 years younger.

If you were to die and come back as a person or thing, what do you think it would be?
Either a great pianist or an accomplished butcher.

If you could choose what to come back as, what would it be?
A beautiful all-purpose talent of any sort.

How would you like to die?
Fast.

What is your motto?
Love the Lord thy God with all thy heart, and soul, and mind—and thy neighbor as thyself.

March 1996
(Child died in 2004.)

The lowest depth of misery: "A dreadful meal badly served."

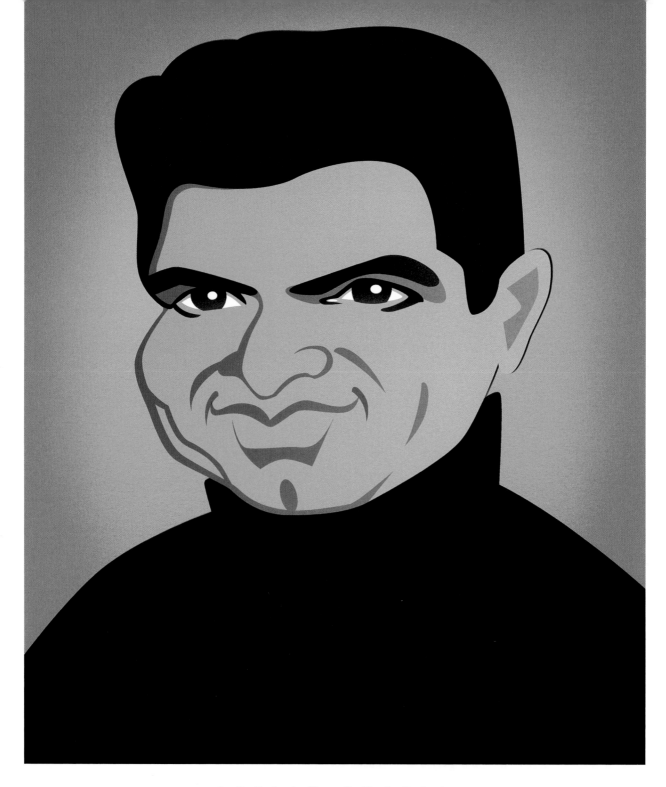

DEEPAK CHOPRA

AUTHOR, SPIRITUAL GUIDE, *and* ALTERNATIVE-MEDICINE EXPERT

My greatest regret: "That I have no regrets to… be nostalgic about."

What is your idea of perfect happiness?
It does not exist. If it did, we'd all be doomed to eternal senility.

What is the trait you most deplore in yourself?
My need for approval.

What is the trait you most deplore in others?
Hypocrisy.

What is your greatest extravagance?
Double hazelnut lattes.

What do you consider the most overrated virtue?
Success.

On what occasion do you lie?
Only when I'm speaking to God.

What do you dislike most about your appearance?
Deepak doesn't believe in evaluating appearances. Deepak likes to be deep.

Which living person do you most despise?
I despise violence and intolerance in all its forms; I gave up despising people a long time ago.

Which words or phrases do you most overuse?
I am impeccable in my use of language.

What is your greatest regret?
That I have no regrets to talk about or be nostalgic about.

Which talent would you most like to have?
To sing like Plácido Domingo.

What do you consider your greatest achievement?
My children.

If you were to die and come back as a person or thing, what do you think it would be?
The breeze.

If you could choose what to come back as, what would it be?
A storm.

What do you regard as the lowest depth of misery?
The hypnosis of social conditioning.

What is your most marked characteristic?
My left, fourth, deformed toe.

Who are your favorite writers?
Somerset Maugham, Rudyard Kipling, T. S. Eliot, George Bernard Shaw, Shakespeare.

Who are your heroes in real life?
Children. In the words of a great Indian poet, "Every child that is born is proof that God has not yet given up on human beings."

What are your favorite names?
The names of my children, Gotham and Mallika.

What is it that you most dislike?
Prejudice and bigotry.

How would you like to die?
In meditation.

What is your motto?
"Don't take yourself seriously."

December 2002

My choice, if I were to be reborn: "A Martin OM-45."

What is your idea of perfect happiness?
Being in the moment.

What is your greatest fear?
Insanity.

Which living person do you most admire?
J. J. Cale.

What is the trait you most deplore in yourself?
Arrogance.

What is the trait you most deplore in others?
Arrogance.

What is your greatest extravagance?
Wristwatches.

What do you consider the most overrated virtue?
Generosity.

What do you dislike most about your appearance?
My eyebrows.

Which living person do you most despise?
Rupert Murdoch.

Which words or phrases do you most overuse?
"Do you know what I mean?"

What is your greatest regret?
Losing my son.

What or who is the greatest love of your life?
My wife and my children.

When and where were you happiest?
On our wedding day.

Which talent would you most like to have?
To be able to paint.

What is your current state of mind?
Contented.

What do you consider your greatest achievement?
Getting sober.

If you could choose what to come back as, what would it be?
A Martin OM-45.

What is your most treasured possession?
My health.

What do you regard as the lowest depth of misery?
Watching English TV.

What is your favorite occupation?
Playing the guitar.

What is your most marked characteristic?
Haste.

What is the quality you most like in a man?
Integrity.

What is the quality you most like in a woman?
Passion.

What do you most value in your friends?
Tolerance.

How would you like to die?
Fishing.

June 2004

ERIC CLAPTON

MUSICIAN

My most overused phrase: "Darling."

What do you consider your greatest achievement?
My Oscar, or still being here at 92.

Which talent would you most like to have?
The ability to turn back the clock.

What is your greatest regret?
At the moment, not to be working.

What is your most marked characteristic?
The left side of my face.

Who was your favorite leading man?
Gary Cooper.

Which words or phrases do you most overuse?
"Darling."

When and where were you happiest?
With my husband, Jack Pressman, in Holmby Hills.

What is your idea of perfect happiness?
Living in Barbados at my home Bellerive by the sea.

What is your favorite journey?
To Bellerive.

What is your most treasured possession?
My beautiful Bellerive.

What is it that you most dislike?
Not having sorbet every day.

What is the trait you most deplore in yourself?
Perfectionism.

What is your greatest fear?
Being alone.

What do you regard as the lowest depth of misery?
Illness.

What is the quality you most like in a man?
A sense of humor.

What is the quality you most like in a woman?
A sense of wit.

What do you most value in your friends?
Loyalty and honesty.

Who is your favorite writer?
Colette.

Who is your favorite hero of fiction?
Snoopy.

Who are your heroes in real life?
My friends.

What is your favorite name?
Tiger Lily, the name of the cat who adopted me.

If you were to die and come back as a person or thing, what do you think it would be?
Cleopatra.

What is your motto?
"To see the 21st century."

April 1996
(Colbert died in July 1996.)

CLAUDETTE COLBERT

ACTRESS

JACKIE COLLINS

WRITER

What is your idea of perfect happiness?
Sitting at my desk with my characters taking me on a wild trip!

What is your greatest fear?
Being held up by a masked gunman. It happened once and I made a daring escape. If it happens again, I think I'd freak!

Which historical figure do you most identify with?
Frank Sinatra. He did it his way.

Which living person do you most admire?
Schoolteachers, doctors, cops. What would we do without them?

What is the trait you most deplore in yourself?
Saying yes when I really want to say no.

What is the trait you most deplore in others?
People who gossip behind your back. If you've got a problem, confront!

What is your favorite journey?
A British Airways flight to London— I take it four times a year.

What do you consider the most overrated virtue?
Piousness.

Which words or phrases do you most overuse?
"Fuckhead"—it's one of my favorites!

What is your greatest regret?
That my mother, Elsa, never lived to see what I was able to achieve.

What or who is the greatest love of your life?
My three incredible daughters.

When and where were you happiest?
Right now. Life's an adventure—you've got to live it every day.

What is your current state of mind?
Sanguine.

If you were to die and come back as a person or thing, what do you think it would be?
A leopard.

If you could choose what to come back as, what would it be?
The first female president—or a leopard!

What is your most treasured possession?
My handwritten manuscripts.

What do you regard as the lowest depth of misery?
Total boredom.

Where would you like to live?
L.A. It's the greatest.

What is your most marked characteristic?
Understanding people's problems— I'd have been a great shrink.

Who are your favorite writers?
F. Scott Fitzgerald, Mario Puzo, Dickens, and Tom Wolfe.

Who is your favorite hero of fiction?
Jay Gatsby.

What are your favorite names?
Lucky, Jade, Montana, and Nick.

What is your motto?
"Girls can do anything!"

June 1999

I deplore: "People who gossip behind your back. If you've got a problem, confront!"

J O A N   C O L L I N S

ACTRESS

My favorite occupation: "Watching a Billy Wilder movie while eating Belgian chocolates."

What is your current state of mind?
Sanguine and reasonably content.

What is your idea of perfect happiness?
Peace—being in my villa in the South of France with my favorite man.

What is your greatest fear?
The thought of being stuck in an elevator in the Beverly Center with everybody watching and no one to bring it down.

What are your favorite names?
Valentino, Karl, Christian, Donna.

Which historical figure do you most identify with?
Marie Antoinette.

What is your greatest extravagance?
Travel and lawyers. The former I adore; the latter, unfortunately, seem to dog me.

What is the trait you most deplore in others?
Those who crave power; they are usually the most dangerous too.

What do you consider the most overrated virtue?
Political correctness.

On what occasion do you lie?
To get out of a boring dinner party.

What is your favorite occupation?
Watching a Billy Wilder movie while eating Belgian chocolates.

What is your greatest regret?
Not to have learnt to speak or write French well enough—I'm still stuck at my 14-year-old level.

What do you consider your greatest achievement?
Apart from my children, to have survived and made an excellent living as an actress for over [50] years is something I'm quite proud of.

What is your most marked characteristic?
Unbridled energy.

What do you most value in your friends?
Loyalty and humor.

Who are your favorite writers?
Oscar Wilde, Jane Austen, John Updike, Truman Capote, Ruth Rendell, Dominick Dunne.

How would you like to die?
With dignity—in my sleep of extreme old age.

If you could choose what to come back as, what would it be?
I would come back as a woman, but with all the knowledge that I have today and the physical strength of a man.

What is your motto?
"That which does not kill us makes us stronger."

January 1995

KATIE COURIC

BROADCAST JOURNALIST

The most overrated virtue: "Inner peace."

What is your idea of perfect happiness?
At the kitchen table, laughing with my daughters.

What is the trait you most deplore in yourself?
I can be a sore loser and an obnoxious winner.

What is the trait you most deplore in others?
Pretentiousness.

What is your greatest extravagance?
My red Thunderbird.

What is your current state of mind?
Exhausted.

What do you consider the most overrated virtue?
Inner peace.

On what occasion do you lie?
My parents don't need to know everything.

What do you dislike most about your appearance?
My chewed-up fingernails.

What is the quality you most like in a man?
Integrity.

What is the quality you most like in a woman?
Humor.

Which living person do you most admire?
Paul Farmer.

Which words or phrases do you most overuse?
"Honestly, you guys . . . "

What or who is the greatest love of your life?
My daughters, Ellie and Carrie.

When and where were you happiest?
I had just brought Carrie home from the hospital, and she, Ellie, and I were taking a nap while my husband, Jay, was playing a Chopin nocturne on the Steinway we had bought each other for our birthdays.

Which talent would you most like to have?
I would sing like Ella Fitzgerald.

If you could change one thing about yourself, what would it be?
I'd grow six inches.

What do you consider your greatest achievement?
Raising awareness about colon cancer.

If you were to die and come back as a person or thing, what do you think it would be?
Thomas Jefferson.

Where would you like to live?
New York City or Tuscany.

What is your most treasured possession?
My grandmother's pillbox collection.

What do you regard as the lowest depth of misery?
Helplessness.

What is your most marked characteristic?
My gummy smile.

Who are your favorite writers?
Edith Wharton, Carson McCullers, Harper Lee, John Steinbeck, Philip Roth.

Who is your favorite hero of fiction?
Mulan.

Which historical figure do you most identify with?
Amelia Earhart.

Who are your heroes in real life?
My parents, cancer researchers, and Dara Torres.

What is your greatest regret?
Not telling my husband I loved him 20 times a day.

How would you like to die?
Quickly.

What is your motto?
"Nobody puts Baby in a corner."

January 2009

WALTER CRONKITE

BROADCAST JOURNALIST

What is your most marked characteristic?
Apparently, from people's reactions, my voice.

When and where were you happiest?
Behind the newsdesk on a fast-breaking story.

What is your idea of perfect happiness?
The post office folds and the fax breaks down.

What do you consider your greatest achievement?
Helping establish some TV news standards.

What is your most treasured possession?
The Presidential Medal of Freedom.

What is your greatest fear?
That terrorists will get a nuclear capability.

Which living person do you most despise?
Any graffiti vandal.

Which living person do you most admire?
Me.

What is the trait you most deplore in yourself?
Humility.

What do you dislike most about your appearance?
Quadruple chin.

Which words or phrases do you most overuse?
"Sounds interesting—call my office."

What is your greatest regret?
Not making a space trip.

What do you regard as the lowest depth of misery?
Death of a loved one, including the family dog.

What is your favorite occupation?
Leading the New York Pops at Carnegie Hall.

What is the quality you most like in a man?
Integrity.

What is the quality you most like in a woman?
I'm strongly urged by advisers not to say "moral laxity," so let's say "sense of humor."

Who are your heroes in real life?
Journalists who face mortal danger in wars and civil insurrection and from corrupt regimes to report the truth.

If you were to die and come back as a person or thing, what do you think it would be?
A seagull—graceful in flight, rapacious in appetite.

If you could choose what to come back as, what would it be?
A favored cat.

How would you like to die?
In my sleep after celebrating the outbreak of permanent world peace.

What is your motto?
Baden-Powell didn't do badly in giving the Boy Scouts "Be prepared."

January 1997
(Cronkite died in 2009.)

I was happiest: "Behind the newsdesk on a fast-breaking story."

My greatest regret: "Most of my marriages."

What is your most marked characteristic?
Optimism.

What do you consider your greatest achievement?
My work with and for the animals.

When and where were you happiest?
My childhood summers in Trenton, Ohio,
and starting work at Warner Bros.

What is your greatest regret?
Most of my marriages.

What is your idea of perfect happiness?
I wish I knew.

What is your most treasured possession?
Each of my pets.

Where would you like to live?
Right here in Carmel, California.

What is your greatest fear?
Flying.

What is the trait you most deplore in yourself?
Perfectionism.

What is the trait you most deplore in others?
Insincerity.

What do you consider the most overrated virtue?
Humility.

What is your greatest extravagance?
The supermarket.

What is your favorite journey?
To the supermarket.

What is it that you most dislike?
Business meetings.

What is the quality you most like in a man?
Honesty.

What is the quality you most like in a woman?
Honesty.

What do you most value in your friends?
Loyalty.

If you were to die and come back as a person or thing, what do you think it would be?
A bird. I always thought it would be wonderful to fly, but not in an airplane.

If you could choose what to come back as, what would it be?
One of my pets.

How would you like to die?
No.

April 1995

D O R I S   D A Y

ACTRESS

ELLEN DeGENERES

COMEDIAN *and* TALK-SHOW HOST

I most value in my friends: "Availability to play poker."

What is your idea of perfect happiness?
I don't know how happiness could get any more perfect, but I think it would involve more puppies.

What is your greatest fear?
Finding a panther in my bathroom.

Which historical figure do you most identify with?
Burt Reynolds.

Which living person do you most admire?
Is Teddy Roosevelt still with us? I liked him. He was a good president.

What is the trait you most deplore in yourself?
That I don't really know the definition of "deplore."

What is the trait you most deplore in others?
Tardiness. No, wait, arrogance. How about being late and then being arrogant about it?

What is your greatest extravagance?
I hope this doesn't affect your opinion of me, but I have a garbage can that you don't even have to touch for it to open. You put your foot in the sensor zone. It's very extravagant.

What is your favorite journey?
Whichever one "Lovin', Touchin', Squeezin'" is on.

What do you consider the most overrated virtue?
Small wrists.

What do you dislike most about your appearance?
My hair can really bug me sometimes.

Which living person do you most despise?
I don't despise anyone. That's a waste of energy.

Which words or phrases do you most overuse?
I say "By Jove!" way too much. Either I do or Sherlock Holmes does. Whoever it is, it has to stop.

What is your greatest regret?
I don't have any regrets or I wouldn't be the person I am today. Although my 80s mullet does come close.

What or who is the greatest love of your life?
PDR.

Which talent would you most like to have?
I'd like to play the piano. Just the black keys.

If you could change one thing about your family, what would it be?
I'm going to save this answer for my memoirs.

What do you consider your greatest achievement?
Being able to do what I love, and being able to install a dimmer.

If you were to die and come back as a person or thing, what do you think it would be?
I've always thought I'd come back as an animal, preferably one that has no predators. So either a tiger or a killer whale. Watch, I'll end up in a SeaWorld with some kid shoving an oversize toothbrush in my mouth.

What do you regard as the lowest depth of misery?
That's a bummer of a question.

What is your most marked characteristic?
I, like Popeye, am what I am.

What do you most value in your friends?
Availability to play poker.

Who are your favorite writers?
My writers.

Who is your favorite hero of fiction?
Madonna and Garp.

What are your favorite names?
Off the top of my head, Tabitha, Darrin . . . let's see . . . Samantha. Basically the whole cast of *Bewitched*. Great fake names.

What is it that you most dislike?
What's with focusing on the negativity?

How would you like to die?
No, thank you.

What is your motto?
"Let's try to beat that."

March 2007

OLIVIA DE HAVILLAND

ACTRESS

I would choose to come back as: "a California redwood."

What is your greatest fear?
The loss of physical, financial, and psychological independence.

Which living person do you most admire?
Nelson Mandela.

What is your greatest extravagance?
Champagne.

What or who is the greatest love of your life?
Change "is" to "are" and the answer is my two children.

When and where were you happiest?
In their company, each of us doing his/her own thing in perfect harmony.

Which talent would you most like to have?
The gift of coolheadedness or the ability to tap-dance.

If you could change one thing about your family, what would it be?
To have my son alive again, happy, healthy, and engaged in the work he loved most.

If you were to die and come back as a person or thing, what do you think it would be?
Person: as me, myself, and I.

If you could choose what to come back as, what would it be?
Thing: as a California redwood tree—tall, strong, deep-rooted, long-living, aromatic, benevolent, reaching toward the sun, the moon, and the stars.

What are your favorite names?
Alexandra and Alexis.

What is your most treasured possession?
The christening cup of Geoffrey Raoul de Havilland, given me by his mother after his death on September 27, 1946, while attempting to break the sound barrier in the DH-108, the de Havilland experimental plane.

What is your favorite occupation?
Doing cryptic crosswords or, equally, reading tales of mystery and imagination.

What is the quality you most like in a man?
Make that plural and the answer is clear-sightedness, humor, fairness, fidelity to purpose.

What is the quality you most like in a woman?
Thoughtfulness.

What is it that you most dislike?
The deception and exploitation of the naïve and defenseless.

How would you like to die?
I would prefer to live forever in perfect health, but if I must at some time leave this life I would like to do so ensconced on a chaise longue, perfumed, wearing a velvet robe and pearl earrings, with a flute of champagne beside me and having just discovered the answer to the last problem in a British cryptic crossword.

What is your motto?
"*Dominus fortissima turris.*" (Variously translated as "God is the strongest tower" or "God is my tower of strength.")

March 2005

My most marked characteristic: "Perseverance."

What is your idea of perfect happiness?
Being at home with my wife, family, dogs, and friends.

What is your greatest fear?
Solitude.

Which living person do you most admire?
My wife.

What is the trait you most deplore in yourself?
Fear.

What is the trait you most deplore in others?
Cowardice.

What is your greatest extravagance?
Living.

On what occasion do you lie?
Only about things that are totally banal to protect others.

What do you dislike most about your appearance?
Not being fit.

Which words or phrases do you most overuse?
"What's new?"

What is your greatest regret?
I have no regrets.

When and where were you happiest?
Now.

If you could change one thing about yourself, what would it be?
My limited attention span.

If you could choose what to come back as, what would it be?
A dog, so that my wife would love me more.

What do you regard as the lowest depth of misery?
Envy.

What is your favorite occupation?
Gardening.

What is your most marked characteristic?
Perseverance.

What is the quality you most like in a man?
Loyalty.

What is the quality you most like in a woman?
Trust.

What do you most value in your friends?
Honesty.

Who are your favorite writers?
Cervantes and Balzac.

Who is your favorite hero of fiction?
Don Quixote.

Who are your heroes in real life?
All those anonymous people who risk their lives fighting for noble causes.

How would you like to die?
In my sleep, dreaming of those I love.

What is your motto?
"Live, love, and laugh."

September 2002

OSCAR DE LA RENTA

FASHION DESIGNER

CATHERINE DENEUVE

ACTRESS

Which historical figure do you most identify with?
George Sand.

Which living person do you most admire?
Aung San Suu Kyi.

What is your greatest fear?
The war.

What is the trait you most deplore in yourself?
Having too many things on my mind at the same time.

What is the trait you most deplore in others?
Inconsistency.

What is your greatest extravagance?
Spending all my money when I was 17 years old to buy an Hermès Kelly bag.

What do you consider the most overrated virtue?
Beauty.

What do you dislike most about your appearance?
My left ear.

Which words or phrases do you most overuse?
"Je ne finis pas mes phrases."
[I do not finish my sentences.]

What or who is the greatest love of your life?
Nature.

Which talent would you most like to have?
The gift of a scientific mind.

What is your current state of mind?
Restless.

If you could change one thing about yourself, what would it be?
My future.

If you could change one thing about your family, what would it be?
Nothing.

What do you consider your greatest achievement?
A wild garden.

If you were to die and come back as a person or thing, what do you think it would be?
A lime tree.

What is your most treasured possession?
Lucidity.

What is your favorite occupation?
Playing in the garden.

What is your most marked characteristic?
Impassivity.

What is the quality you most like in a man?
Fantasy and talent.

What do you most value in your friends?
Uniqueness.

Who are your favorite writers?
Rainer Maria Rilke.

Who is your favorite hero of fiction?
Mandrake the Magician.

What is it that you most dislike?
Insects.

How would you like to die?
In my sleep or standing.

What is your motto?
"À coeur vaillant, rien d'impossible."
[With a valiant heart, nothing is impossible.]

January 2006

"With a valiant heart, nothing is impossible."

JOAN DIDION

WRITER

"In retrospect she seemed to have been most happy in borrowed houses, and at lunch."

What is your greatest fear?

I have an irrational fear of snakes. When my husband and I moved to a part of Los Angeles County with many rattlesnakes, I tried to desensitize myself by driving every day to a place called Hermosa Reptile Import-Export and forcing myself to watch the anacondas. This seemed to work, but a few years later, when we were living in Malibu and I had a Corvette, a king snake (a "good" snake, not poisonous, by no means anaconda-like) dropped from a garage rafter into the car. My daughter, then four, brought it to show me. I am ashamed to say I ran away. I still think about what would have happened had I driven to the market and noticed my passenger, the snake, on the Pacific Coast Highway.

What is the trait you most deplore in yourself?

I procrastinate. I play computer solitaire. I fall into depressive sloth. I don't like it, but there it is.

What do you consider the most overrated virtue?

I find "speaking one's mind" pretty overrated, in that it usually turns out to be a way of aggrandizing the speaker at the expense of the helpless listener.

What is your favorite journey?

A long time ago, before they showed movies on airplanes and decided to make you close the blinds, I used to love flying west and watching the country open up, the checkerboarded farms of the Midwest giving way to the vast stretches of nothing. I also loved flying over the Pole from Europe to Los Angeles during the day, when you could see ice floes and islands in the sea change almost imperceptibly to lakes in the land. This shift in perception was very thrilling to me.

On what occasion do you lie?

I probably lie constantly, if the definition of lying includes white lies, social lies, lies to ease a situation or make someone feel better. My mother was incapable of lying. I remember her driving into a blinding storm to vote for an acquaintance in an S.P.C.A. election. "I told Dorothy I would," she said when I tried to dissuade her. "How will Dorothy know?" I asked. "That's not the point," my mother said. I'm sorry to report that this was amazing to me.

CONTINUED ON PAGE 72 >

JOAN DIDION

WRITER

‹ CONTINUED FROM PAGE 71

What do you dislike most about your appearance?
For a while there I disliked being short, but I got used to it. Which is not to say I wouldn't have preferred to be five-ten and get sent clothes by designers.

Which words or phrases do you most overuse?
Most people who write find themselves overusing certain words or constructions (if they worked once, they then get hardwired), so much so that a real part of the exercise is getting those repetitions out.

When and where were you happiest?
Once, in a novel, *Democracy,* I had the main character, Inez Victor, consider this very question, which was hard for her. She drinks her coffee, she smokes a cigarette, she thinks it over, she comes to a conclusion: "In retrospect she seemed to have been most happy in borrowed houses, and at lunch. She recalled being extremely happy eating lunch by herself in a hotel room in Chicago, once when snow was drifting on the window ledges. There was a lunch in Paris that she remembered in detail: a late lunch with Harry and the twins at Pré Catelan in the rain." These lunches and borrowed houses didn't come from nowhere.

What talent would you most like to have?
I long to be fluent in languages other than English. I am resigned to the fact that this will not happen. A lot of things get in the way, not least a stubborn fear of losing my only real asset since childhood, the ability to put English sentences together.

If you could change one thing about yourself, what would it be?
I'm afraid that "one thing" would just lead to another thing, making this a question only the truly greedy would try to answer.

What is your most treasured possession?
I treasure things my daughter has given me, for example (I think of this because it is always on my desk), a picture book called *Baby Animals and Their Mothers.*

What do you regard as the lowest depth of misery?
Misery is feeling estranged from people I love. Misery is also not working. The two seem to go together.

"She [was] extremely happy eating lunch by herself in a hotel room in Chicago, once when snow was drifting on the window ledges."

Where would you like to live?

I want to live somewhere else every month or so. Right now I would like to be living on Kailua Beach, on the windward side of Oahu. Around November, I'm quite sure I will want to be living in Paris, preferably in the Hotel Bristol. I like hotels a lot. When we were living in houses in Los Angeles I used to make charts showing how we could save money by living in a bungalow at the Bel-Air, but my husband never bought it.

What is your favorite occupation?

I like making gumbo. I like gardening. I like writing, at least when it's going well, maybe because it seems to be exactly as tactile a thing to do as making gumbo or gardening.

What is your most marked characteristic?

If I listened to other people, I would think my most marked characteristic was being thin. What strikes me about myself, however, is not my thinness but a certain remoteness. I tune out a lot.

Who is your favorite hero of fiction?

Axel Heyst in Joseph Conrad's *Victory* has always attracted me as a character. Standing out on that dock in, I think (I may be wrong, because I have no memory), Sumatra. His great venture, the Tropical Belt Coal Company, gone to ruin behind him. And then he does something so impossibly brave that he can only be doing it because he has passed entirely beyond concern for himself.

October 2003

KIRK DOUGLAS

ACTOR

The aspect of my appearance I most dislike: "My chin."

What is your greatest fear?
That I will lose my speech.

Which historical figure do you most identify with?
Moses.

Which living person do you most admire?
President Jimmy Carter.

What is the trait you most deplore in yourself?
Impatience.

What is the trait you most deplore in others?
Lack of punctuality.

What is your greatest extravagance?
My wife.

What is your favorite journey?
To our house in Montecito.

What do you consider the most overrated virtue?
Being too religious.

On what occasion do you lie?
When I don't want to hurt someone's feelings.

What do you dislike most about your appearance?
My chin.

Which words or phrases do you most overuse?
"You know … "

What is your greatest regret?
That I have not paid attention to friendships in the past.

What or who is the greatest love of your life?
My wife, Anne.

If you could change one thing about yourself, what would it be?
Get my speech back to what it was.

If you could change one thing about your family, what would it be?
To get together more often.

What do you consider your greatest achievement?
Breaking the blacklist by using Dalton Trumbo's name on *Spartacus*.

If you were to die and come back as a person or thing, what do you think it would be?
The second husband of my wife.

What do you regard as the lowest depth of misery?
Having a stroke.

What do you most value in your friends?
Loyalty.

Who is your favorite hero of fiction?
Don Quixote.

What is it that you most dislike?
People who have more than others but don't give.

How would you like to die?
In my sleep.

What is your motto?
"I tried, goddammit, I tried!"

January 2002

My greatest regret: "Lipstick traces."

Which historical figure do you most identify with?
Madame X.

What is your greatest extravagance?
Bringing unnecessary presents for unnecessary men.

What is your favorite journey?
Pago Pago (if only Dan Quayle hadn't been along).

What do you consider the most overrated virtue?
Gravitas.

On what occasion do you lie?
On Proust Questionnaires.

What do you dislike most about your appearance?
The upkeep.

Which words or phrases do you most overuse?
"Chuckleheaded presidential cronies."

What is your greatest regret?
Lipstick traces.

What or who is the greatest love of your life?
You'll be the first to know.

If you could change one thing about yourself, what would it be?
My credit report.

What do you consider your greatest achievement?
Covering six presidential campaigns in heels.

If you could choose what to come back as, what would it be?
Jane Greer in *Out of the Past*.

If you were to die and come back as a person or thing, what do you think it would be?
A crisp, perfectly salted French fry.

What is your most treasured possession?
My sanity.

What do you regard as the lowest depth of misery?
No mini-bar.

Where would you like to live?
Chateau Marmont, Room 64.

What is your favorite occupation?
Anything but the occupation of Iraq.

What is the quality you most like in a man?
Patience.

What is the quality you most like in a woman?
Impatience.

What do you most value in your friends?
Availability at deadline.

Who are your favorite writers?
Jean Rhys and Preston Sturges.

Who are your heroes in real life?
The personal assistants of famous people.

What are your favorite names?
Rummy, Wolfie, and Brownie.

How would you like to die?
After my enemies.

What is your motto?
"When blue, wear red."

December 2005

MAUREEN DOWD

COLUMNIST

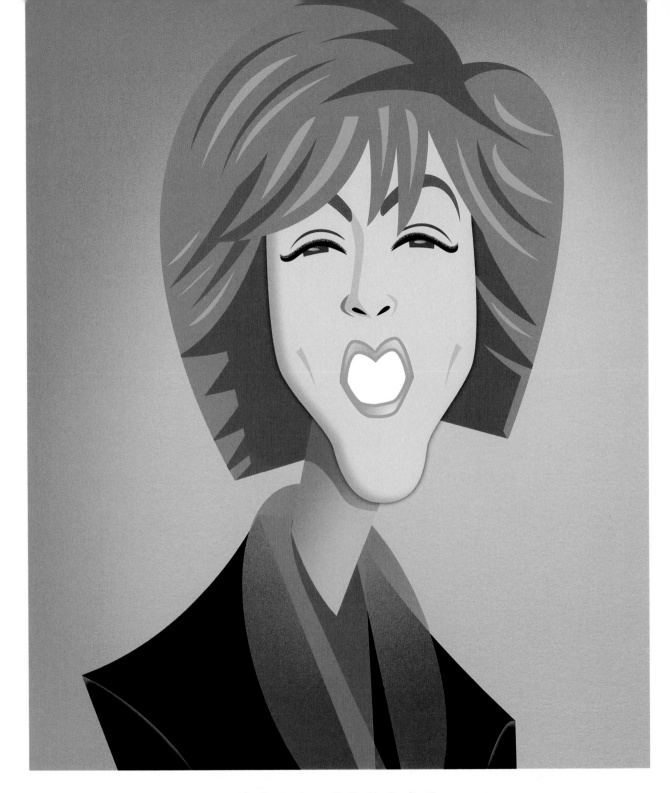

NORA EPHRON

AUTHOR, SCREENWRITER, *and* DIRECTOR

The trait I most deplore in myself: "My inability to resist a questionnaire."

What is the trait you most deplore in yourself?
My inability to resist a questionnaire.

What is your current state of mind?
Unleaded.

What is your idea of perfect happiness?
Meeting my friends for dinner in a city where none of us lives.

When and where were you happiest?
Almost always in Las Vegas. And East Hampton in the summer of 1993.

Which living person do you most admire?
My husband.

What is your favorite journey?
Coming home to Manhattan over the Triborough Bridge on a clear night.

What do you consider your greatest achievement?
My ability to cook dinner for a large number of people in a short space of time.

What is your greatest fear?
A dental emergency in a Third World country.

What is it that you most dislike?
Going to the symphony.

What is your greatest regret?
Not having bought a very nice apartment on 75th Street between Lex and Third in 1976.

Where would you like to live?
Overlooking Central Park.

Which talent would you most like to have?
If only I could sing.

Which words or phrases do you most overuse?
"Um" and "you know."

What is the quality you most like in a man?
Manliness.

What is the quality you most like in a woman?
Manliness.

What do you most value in your friends?
Discretion and the fact that none of them ever calls me after 11 at night.

Who are your favorite writers?
Jane Austen and Charles Dickens. Wilkie Collins is not my favorite writer, but he once wrote one of my favorite books, *The Woman in White*.

Who is your favorite hero of fiction?
Billina.

How would you like to die?
In my sleep, at age 84, after dinner at L'Ami Louis.

What is your motto?
"You never know."

December 1996

I would choose to come back as: "Shirley MacLaine's handbag."

What is your idea of perfect happiness?
I don't think there is any such thing.

What is your greatest fear?
A bad death . . . fast or slow.

Which historical figure do you most identify with?
Mad King George's psychiatrist.

Which living person do you most admire?
David Spade's assistant.

What is the trait you most deplore in yourself?
My driving skills.

What is your greatest extravagance?
Antique jewelry and medieval stained glass.

On what occasion do you lie?
When I have been high.

What do you dislike most about your appearance?
My head. It looks like either an egg with hair or a bowl of oatmeal with features.

Which living person do you most despise?
A certain Republican . . . who will remain nameless.

What or who is the greatest love of your life?
Cary Grant.

When and where were you happiest?
In my manic highs, which are too numerous to mention.

Which talent would you most like to have?
Dieting.

What do you consider your greatest achievement?
My child and certain areas of my personality.

What is your current state of mind?
New York.

If you could change one thing about yourself, what would it be?
My inability to have romantic relationships.

If you could change one thing about your family, what would it be?
More kids like the one I got, and my father's book.

If you were to die and come back as a person or thing, what do you think it would be?
A stone, a leaf, or an unfound door.

If you could choose what to come back as, what would it be?
Shirley MacLaine's handbag.

What is your most treasured possession?
My Muller Frères lamp.

What do you regard as the lowest depth of misery?
My psychotic episode, or dinner with a conservative.

Where would you like to live?
London.

What is your favorite occupation?
Conversationalist.

What is your most marked characteristic?
Large life.

What do you most value in your friends?
A well-stocked medicine cabinet.

Who are your favorite writers?
Salman Rushdie, Bruce Wagner, George Eliot.

Who are your heroes in life?
My mother.

What is it that you most dislike?
Pain and aging.

How would you like to die?
Morphine home care.

What is your motto?
"Fuck that shit."

April 2001

CARRIE FISHER
ACTRESS and WRITER

JANE FONDA

ACTRESS

I would like to change: "My inability to have a long-term intimate relationship."

What is your idea of perfect happiness?
Being totally present and at peace in the moment—and knowing that my children and grandchildren are all right.

What is your greatest fear?
That we won't act fast enough to save the planet.

What is the trait you most deplore in yourself?
The tendency to withdraw into myself.

What is the trait you most deplore in others?
Cynicism.

What is your greatest extravagance?
Buying large trees to place around my ranch house. (I am too old for saplings.)

What is your current state of mind?
Acceptance.

On what occasion do you lie?
When the truth will serve no purpose and only hurt.

What do you dislike most about your appearance?
My naked self in an overhead light.

Which living person do you most despise?
Cheney, Rumsfeld, and Kissinger—just about equally—for their cynicism and disdain for life.

What do you most value in your friends?
Honesty.

What or who is the greatest love of your life?
My children and grandchildren.

When and where were you happiest?
Hiking to the top of a 14,000-foot mountain.

If you could change one thing about yourself, what would it be?
My inability to have a long-term intimate relationship.

What do you consider your greatest achievement?
Never settling for what is, but striving for "What if . . . ?"

Where would you like to live?
Right where I am.

What is your most treasured possession?
My ranch and its ever changing wildness.

What is your favorite occupation?
Mountain climbing.

What is your most marked characteristic?
Being down to earth.

Who are your favorite writers?
Proust, Shakespeare.

Which historical figure do you most identify with?
Abraham Lincoln.

What is it that you most dislike?
A lack of compassion.

What is your greatest regret?
Regrets are a waste of time except as things to learn from.

Which talent would you most like to have?
To be able to sing.

How would you like to die?
In my home, in bed, surrounded by my family. I can see it all quite clearly, and I am not afraid of it.

What is your motto?
"It's better to be interested than interesting."

May 2009

The most overrated virtue: "Virginity."

What is your idea of perfect happiness?
Working in my garden while my five A.S.P.C.A. dogs smell the roses . . . or water them.

What is your greatest fear?
As I lost my Brentwood, California, house and its contents in a firestorm in 1964, I fear the same might happen to Villa Fontana.

Which historical figure do you most identify with?
Eleanor of Aquitaine, as she was my all-time favorite role, in *The Lion in Winter,* and which gave me the best reviews of my career.

What is your greatest extravagance?
Buying a car just for my canines.

What is your favorite journey?
Portofino to Capri.

What do you consider the most overrated virtue?
Virginity.

On what occasion do you lie?
When being tactful . . . or evasive.

Which words or phrases do you most overuse?
"Ah!"

What or who is the greatest love of your life?
The English language.

What is your current state of mind?
Contentment.

If you could change one thing about yourself, what would it be?
Recklessness.

What is the trait you most deplore in yourself?
Impulsiveness.

What is the trait you most deplore in others?
Gossiping, denigration, chitchat, disloyalty.

What do you consider your greatest achievement?
Peace and tranquillity.

What do you regard as the lowest depth of misery?
Losing a child.

What is your most treasured possession?
My house and its three acres of gardens, in the woods.

What is your most marked characteristic?
Independence, sense of humor.

What is the quality you most like in a man?
Knowledge and respect, affection without demands.

What is the quality you most like in a woman?
Intellect, honesty, openness, loyalty.

Who are your favorite writers?
Du Maurier, Shakespeare, Dickens, the Brontës, Gwendolyn Brooks.

Who is your favorite hero of fiction?
D'Artagnan, from *The Three Musketeers,* who taught me some things were going on in Milady's boudoir. My mother, when I questioned her at 10 years old, said, "You'll have to ask someone else."

Who are your heroes in real life?
Winston Churchill. Alas, no "greats" today, except Mother Teresa.

If you were to die and come back as a person or thing, what do you think it would be?
Me again. "Get it *right* this time!"

What is it that you most dislike?
Noise.

How would you like to die?
In bed—alone.

What is your motto?
"Free at last!"

March 2008

JOAN FONTAINE

ACTRESS

What is your idea of perfect happiness?
It's never going to be absolutely perfect. There will always be something you would change if you could.

What is your greatest fear?
My lips are sealed.

What is your favorite journey?
There are multiple, such as the journey of recording a song or the journey of performing onstage.

Which words or phrases do you most overuse?
"You know what I'm sayin'."

What is your greatest regret?
Not learning to read music. However, Juilliard is still on my mind! I've come within two blocks of the building, and my schedule would not allow for me to enroll at the time.

What or who is the greatest love of your life?
Wouldn't you like to know!

When and where were you happiest?
Right here, right now.

Which talent would you most like to have?
I have it. Thank God!

If you could change one thing about yourself, what would it be?
My weight, but I'm working on it. I will return!

Where would you like to live?
Where I live.

What is your favorite occupation?
Being a singer/performer.

What is the quality you most like in a man?
Straight-up honesty and good taste.

What is the quality you most like in a woman?
Honesty, style, and realness.

Who are your favorite writers?
I enjoy reading about people such as Quincy Jones, Della Reese, and of course my own autobiography, *Aretha: From These Roots*. My all-time favorite musical writers are Holland, Dozier, and Holland; Michael Masser; L.A. and Babyface; Smokey Robinson; and myself, among others.

Who are your heroes in real life?
My dad. I also appreciate the accomplishments of Congresswomen Barbara Jordan and Maxine Waters, Lena Horne, Ella Fitzgerald, Bette Davis, Cicely Tyson, Barbara Stanwyck, Ingrid Bergman, Berry Gordy, John H. Johnson, and Franklin Raines. Also, the heroes of the civil-rights movement—who were and are interested in dignity for everyone—such as Julian Bond, Jesse Jackson, Benjamin Hooks, Dr. Martin Luther King Jr., and so many others. These are terrifically courageous and deep people.

What are your favorite names?
Franklin, natch. However, I'm not stuck on myself or the family name.

What is it that you most dislike?
Bad manners.

What is your motto?
"Live and let live!"

November 2003

The quality I most like in a man: "Straight-up honesty and good taste."

ARETHA FRANKLIN

SINGER

ALLEN GINSBERG

POET

My most marked characteristic: "Incriminating eloquence."

What is your idea of perfect happiness?
Excellent health, no flu, no leprosy.

What is your most marked characteristic?
Incriminating eloquence.

What is your greatest extravagance?
Poetry office with fax, Xerox, and photography archive.

What is your favorite occupation?
Writing poems in a bedside notebook.

What is the trait you most deplore in others?
Insanity, drug-induced or natural.

What is your greatest regret?
I didn't accept a friend's invitation to
get in bed naked in 1944.

What is the trait you most deplore in yourself?
Continuous cowardice.

**If you could change one thing about yourself,
what would it be?**
Renew my body, set at 17.

Which living person do you most despise?
New York City's Cardinal O'Connor, for his gay
hypocrisy, considering that his powerful predecessor
Cardinal Spellman was notoriously gay.

On what occasion do you lie?
To protect my friends from my public life in poetry.
Candor for oneself doesn't require snitching on others.

What do you consider the most overrated virtue?
Virginity and/or cynicism and/or machismo.

What do you regard as the lowest depth of misery?
Co-dependency with madman or -woman.

What is the quality you most like in a man?
Intelligent beauty.

What is the quality you most like in a woman?
Sympathetic self-reliability.

Who is your favorite hero of fiction?
Prince Myshkin in Dostoyevsky's *The Idiot*.

Who are your heroes in real life?
William Seward Burroughs, Tibetan lama Nawang Gelek
Rinpoche, sensei Philip Whalen, Bob Dylan.

What is your favorite journey?
To Benares, the "oldest continuously inhabited
city in the world."

Where would you like to live?
Sometimes in Paris, sometimes London, sometimes
Benares, sometimes San Francisco, sometimes New York.

How would you like to die?
In Buddhist community, peacefully,
aged 100, in the presence of a helpful lama.

What is your motto?
"First thought, best thought."

**If you were to die and come back as a person or thing,
what do you think it would be?**
The Eiffel Tower.

What is it that you most dislike?
Theopolitical nationalist "family values" TV hypocrites
and their corresponding heads of state.

Which words or phrases do you most overuse?
"Situation," "sitting practice of meditation,"
and "Beat Generation."

March 1994
(Ginsberg died in 1997.)

JANE GOODALL

PRIMATOLOGIST *and* ENVIRONMENTALIST

"As thy days, so shall thy strength be."

What is your idea of perfect happiness?
Sitting by myself in the forest in Gombe National Park watching one of the chimpanzee mothers with her family.

What is your greatest fear?
That I shall be tortured and be a coward.

What is the trait you most deplore in others?
Hypocrisy.

What is your greatest extravagance?
Long-distance phone calls to my friends.

What is your favorite journey?
My favorite ever journey was my first trip from Nairobi City to the Serengeti to Olduvai Gorge before it was famous, when there were no roads and all the animals were there. We were in an overloaded Land Rover, four people and two Dalmatians.

What do you dislike most about your appearance?
Aging skin!

What or who is the greatest love of your life?
My childhood companion and teacher—my dog, Rusty.

When and where were you happiest?
The early 60s, when I was alone at Gombe with the chimpanzees.

Which talent would you most like to have?
Ability to learn languages.

What is your current state of mind?
Deep concern at the state of the planet, environmental and social.

If you could change one thing about yourself, what would it be?
I need to be 20 years younger—there is too much to do.

What do you consider your greatest achievement?
Starting our youth program, Roots & Shoots, along with helping to blur the line between humans and the rest of the animal kingdom.

What do you regard as the lowest depth of misery?
Knowing you have let someone down, betrayed their trust.

What is your favorite occupation?
Observing animals alone in the wilderness.

What is your most marked characteristic?
Determination/optimism.

What do you most value in your friends?
Being able to share happiness and sadness and have a good laugh.

Who are your favorite writers?
Shakespeare, Tolkien, Mary Wesley.

Who is your favorite hero of fiction?
Robin Hood.

Who are your heroes in real life?
My mother, until her death; dedicated teachers; Kofi Annan; Nelson Mandela; Muhammad Yunus.

What is it that you most dislike?
Receptions and dinners in noisy places with people talking too loud, riding in stretch limos, waste.

How would you like to die?
Peacefully and before losing my physical and especially my mental facilities.

What is your motto?
"As thy days, so shall thy strength be."

May 2004

"The readiness is all."
—*Hamlet*, Act V.

When and where were you happiest?
Now. And here.

What is your idea of perfect happiness?
A real love of the world and all the people and animals in it.

What or who is the greatest love of your life?
My wife, Merula, of course, and my dog Walter, a Dandie Dinmont terrier, now dead.

What is your current state of mind?
So-so.

Which talent would you most like to have?
To take a genuine and charming interest in other people.

If you could change one thing about yourself, what would it be?
I'd like to get rid of my impatience.

If you could change one thing about your family, what would it be?
Their financial situation.

What do you consider your greatest achievement?
Getting through the 1939–45 war pretending to be a naval officer.

What is your most treasured possession?
A cheap pocket compass that belonged to Dr. Wilson and which he took on Scott's last expedition to the South Pole.

Where would you like to live?
Perfectly happy where I am, except for the noise of the traffic.

What is your greatest fear?
Senile dementia.

What is the trait you most deplore in yourself?
Evasiveness.

What is the trait you most deplore in others?
Flattery.

What is it that you most dislike?
Cruelty in all its forms.

What is your greatest extravagance?
Neckties from Hermès.

What is your favorite journey?
Anywhere through northern or central Italy.

What do you consider the most overrated virtue?
Political correctness.

On what occasion do you lie?
To excuse myself from functions I don't wish to attend.

What do you dislike most about your appearance?
The look of weakness and seeking to please I catch in my face.

Which living person do you most despise?
I despise none, but I dislike most politicians.

Which words or phrases do you most overuse?
"That reminds me … "

What is your most marked characteristic?
Restlessness, followed by slothfulness.

What is your greatest regret?
Signing a film contract to make four films.

What is your favorite occupation?
Idly chatting out-of-doors on a summer evening with a long, cold drink in my hand.

What do you most value in your friends?
Their capacity to listen sympathetically.

Who are your heroes in real life?
Robert Louis Stevenson and Cardinal Basil Hume, Archbishop of Westminster.

If you were to die and come back as a person or thing, what do you think it would be?
An unlikely event.

How would you like to die?
Without a struggle.

What is your motto?
"The readiness is all."—*Hamlet*, Act V.

*August 1997
(Guinness died in 2000.)*

ALEC GUINNESS

ACTOR

HUGH HEFNER

EDITOR *and* PUBLISHER

What is your idea of perfect happiness?
To love and be loved.

What is your greatest fear?
To not be able to die in your own time, on your own terms.

Which historical figure do you most identify with?
Hugh Hefner, of course.

What is the trait you most deplore in yourself?
Impatience.

What is your greatest extravagance?
My girlfriends.

What is your favorite journey?
Going to bed with someone I love.

What do you consider the most overrated virtue?
Prudery.

What do you dislike most about your appearance?
I like my appearance. It has aged well.

Which words or phrases do you most overuse?
"Fucking incredible!" "Cut to the chase!"

What is your greatest regret?
That it will one day be over.

Which talent would you most like to have?
To sing like Frank Sinatra.

What is your current state of mind?
Happier than anyone deserves.

If you could change one thing about yourself, what would it be?
My age. I'd like another 50 years.

If you could change one thing about your family, what would it be?
More affection when I was young.

What do you consider your greatest achievement?
The creation of *Playboy* magazine and the influence it has had on society.

What is your most treasured possession?
My memories.

What do you regard as the lowest depth of misery?
Unrequited love.

Where would you like to live?
Here at the Playboy Mansion.

What is the quality you most like in a man?
A lack of hypocrisy.

What is the quality you most like in a woman?
Sincerity and passion.

What do you most value in your friends?
Character and similar interests.

Who are your favorite writers?
Edgar Allan Poe when I was a boy.
F. Scott Fitzgerald when I was a young man.

Who is your favorite hero of fiction?
Sherlock Holmes.

What are your favorite names?
Brande, Sandy, and Mandy.

How would you like to die?
In my sleep.

What is your motto?
"This above all: to thine own self be true."

September 2000

The lowest depth of misery: "Unrequited love."

CAROLINA HERRERA

FASHION DESIGNER

The occasion when I lie: "Whenever I have to… It is called manners."

What is your idea of perfect happiness?
Perfection does not exist—only God is perfect.

What is your greatest fear?
The loss of memories.

What is the trait you most deplore in yourself?
Impatience.

What is the trait you most deplore in others?
Envy.

What is your greatest extravagance?
The waste of time.

What is your current state of mind?
Sunny but with a few clouds here and there.

What do you consider the most overrated virtue?
Virtue.

On what occasion do you lie?
Whenever I have to … It is called manners.

Which living person do you most despise?
Anyone who abuses a child.

What is the quality you most like in a man?
A man has to have sensibility, wit, mystery, tolerance, and strength … Romance also helps.

What is the quality you most like in a woman?
Loyalty.

Which words or phrases do you most overuse?
"If."

What or who is the greatest love of your life?
Fortunately, my husband.

When and where were you happiest?
In many stages of my life.

Which talent would you most like to have?
To be able to read the minds of other people.

If you could change one thing about yourself, what would it be?
I would like to have much greater knowledge.

What do you consider your greatest achievement?
My children.

If you were to die and come back as a person or thing, what do you think it would be?
Carolina Herrera.

What is your most treasured possession?
My imagination, which allows me to create a world of fantasy.

What do you regard as the lowest depth of misery?
The suffering of someone you love.

What is your most marked characteristic?
Curiosity.

What do you most value in your friends?
The ability to make one laugh.

Who are your heroes in real life?
The unknown people who make the world safer: nurses, researchers, doctors, teachers, etc., etc.

What is it that you most dislike?
Cruelty.

What is your greatest regret?
Things that I could have done but didn't.

How would you like to die?
In peace, with my eyes open, waiting for the next great adventure.

What is your motto?
"Always leave room for fantasy."

September 2008

My most overused phrase: "How was yours?"

What is your idea of perfect happiness?
When the coffee kicks in early in the morning and I'm on the couch with my dogs, reading the paper.

What is your greatest fear?
My belief that saying it makes it happen.

Which living person do you most admire?
The Portuguese director Manoel de Oliveira, who is 100 years old and still working.

What is your greatest extravagance?
Disposable glasses.

What do you consider the most overrated virtue?
Moderation.

On what occasion do you lie?
When people ask, "How are you?" The real answer I save for my therapist.

What do you dislike most about your appearance?
That it is only skin-deep.

Which living person do you most despise?
Any bully.

What is the quality you most like in a man?
Non-threatening.

What is the quality you most like in a woman?
Threatening.

Which words or phrases do you most overuse?
"How was yours?"

What or who is the greatest love of your life?
My family, which keeps growing.

When and where were you happiest?
The moment I knew I would spend my life with Lisa.

Which talent would you most like to have?
To play good jazz piano.

If you could change one thing about yourself, what would it be?
I'd like to read faster.

What do you consider your greatest achievement?
Knowing how much I don't know.

What is your most treasured possession?
My notebooks.

What do you most value in your friends?
Private planes.

What do you regard as the lowest depth of misery?
Auditioning.

What is your favorite occupation?
Eavesdropping.

What is your most marked characteristic?
Unpredictability. However, those who know me find me very predictable.

Who are your favorite writers?
Nineteenth-century Russians.

Who is your favorite hero of fiction?
Mr. Magoo.

Which historical figure do you most identify with?
Columbus—if it's true that he knew where he was going, got lost, and found a place that was better.

Who are your heroes in real life?
Those who overcome adversity.

What is your greatest regret?
Waiting too long to do those things that I'm finally hoping to do now.

What is your motto?
"The true mystery of the world is the visible, not the invisible." —Oscar Wilde

February 2009

DUSTIN HOFFMAN

ACTOR

DENNIS HOPPER

ACTOR *and* FILMMAKER

What is your idea of perfect happiness?
Not having a thought in my mind.

Which historical figure do you most identify with?
God.

Which living person do you most admire?
God.

What is the trait you most deplore in yourself?
God worship.

What is your favorite occupation?
Still photography.

What is your most marked characteristic?
My work ethic.

Which talent would you most like to have?
Singing.

What or who is the greatest love of your life?
Film directing and acting.

If you could change one thing about yourself, what would it be?
Get better parts.

If you could change one thing about your family, what would it be?
That my son could live full-time with me.

Who is your favorite hero of fiction?
Guy Grand from *The Magic Christian*.

Who are your heroes in real life?
All the so-and-sos who got fed up and changed things.

What is your most treasured possession?
My collection of mothballs.

What do you regard as the lowest depth of misery?
O. J. Simpson.

What is the quality you most like in a man?
A strong stillness.

What is the quality you most like in a woman?
Feminine strength.

What are your favorite names?
Hey, you.

What do you consider your greatest achievement?
Survival living.

What is your greatest fear?
Death.

What is your greatest regret?
Mortality—that you don't live forever.

If you were to die and come back as a person or thing, what do you think it would be?
A fighting bull.

If you could choose what to come back as, what would it be?
A matador.

How would you like to die?
With my boots on.

What is your motto?
"Never wear boots."

November 1996

How I would like to die: "With my boots on." My motto: "Never wear boots."

RON HOWARD

ACTOR, DIRECTOR, *and* PRODUCER

"Save the drama for the spotlight, people."

What is your idea of perfect happiness?
I don't believe in perfection, but those acrimony-free gaps during our family holidays can be downright blissful.

Which historical figure do you most identify with?
Lenny Wilkins. A long career as a point guard, a longer career as a head coach.

Which living person do you most admire?
My father, who at 19 had the courage to change the course of his family's history by damning logic, leaving the farm, and coming to Hollywood to be in "the show business."

What is the trait you most deplore in yourself?
Emotional reliance on other people's approval.

What is your favorite journey?
The journey of discovery that every film project entails.

What do you consider the most overrated virtue?
Trendiness.

On what occasion do you lie?
When young kids ask about Santa Claus.

What do you dislike most about your appearance?
It's a tie between the gap-toothed grin framed with big ears and the round-shouldered, bowlegged slouch.

Which living person do you most despise?
Joseph Kony, the Ugandan rebel leader.

What or who is the greatest love of your life?
My wife, Cheryl. Hands down, and I've had a lot of love in my life.

When and where were you happiest?
The delivery room for the birth of my kids, standing at the altar watching Cheryl walk down the aisle, and the wrap party of the first film I directed, at 23.

Which talent would you most like to have?
Spontaneous wit. I always think of the good comebacks on the car ride home.

If you could change one thing about your family, what would it be?
Save the drama for the spotlight, people.

What do you consider your greatest achievement?
Forty-eight consecutive years of steady employment in television and film, while preserving a rich family life.

If you were to die and come back as a person or thing, what do you think it would be?
A woman. My wife keeps wishing that upon me, and I find she often gets what she wants.

If you could choose what to come back as, what would it be?
One of those hyper-observant extraterrestrials that occasionally swing by planet Earth.

What is your most treasured possession?
The Oscar for best director.

What is your most marked characteristic?
Patience.

Who are your favorite writers?
The *Daily Show with Jon Stewart* staff.

Who is your favorite hero of fiction?
R. P. McMurphy, of *One Flew over the Cuckoo's Nest.*

What is it that you most dislike?
Firing people.

What is your motto?
"Panic is not our friend."

June 2006

JASPER JOHNS

ARTIST

The most overrated virtue: "virtue itself."

What is your idea of perfect happiness?
I am not strong on perfection

What is your greatest extravagance?
a frugality that seems to confuse people who work with me

What is your current state of mind?
something like very slow panic

What is the trait you most deplore in yourself?
desire for approval

What is the trait you most deplore in others?
the tendency toward self-description

What do you consider the most overrated virtue?
virtue itself

What is your favorite occupation?
painting

What is your most marked characteristic?
never knowing whether to expand or contract

What do you most value in your friends?
tolerance, I suppose

When and where were you happiest?
Pearl Street in 1950s NYC, but memory distorts

What do you dislike most about your appearance?
what I imagine to be the general effect

Which living person do you most despise?
there is none

On what occasion do you lie?
when I think it is useful

What or who is the greatest love of your life?
no one, no thing

Which talent would you most like to have?
the ability to remember or forget at will

If you could change one thing about yourself, what would it be?
my inability to sing or dance

If you could change one thing about your family, what would it be?
no one thing would do the trick

What is your most treasured possession?
my refrigerator

What do you regard as the lowest depth of misery?
intolerable pain of any sort

Who are your favorite writers?
among them, Freud, Helen Keller, Edwin Arlington Robinson

Who is your favorite hero of fiction?
Jack (be nimble)

Who are your heroes in real life?
dead artists and, a few, alive

What are your favorite names?
William, Mary, Augusta

What is it that you most dislike?
seeing fish with silver skin marinating in cream

What do you consider your greatest achievement?
only my work suggests, perhaps wrongly, an effort in that direction

If you were to die and come back as a person or thing, what do you think it would be?
unlikely

If you could choose what to come back as, what would it be?
must I decide *before* I die

Where would you like to live?
not in the past

How would you like to die?
effortlessly

What is your greatest regret?
an absence of clarity

What is your motto?
I have none

December 2007

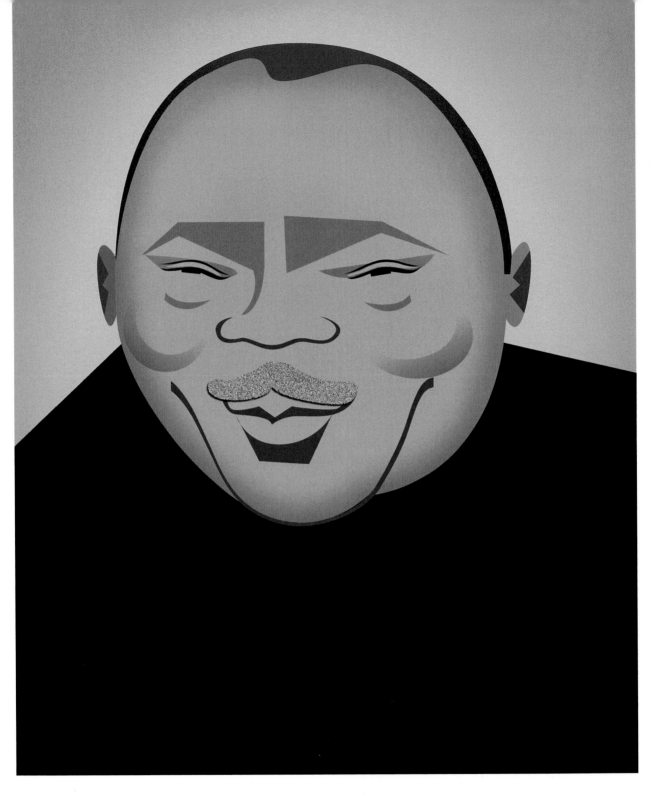

QUINCY JONES

MUSICIAN *and* PRODUCER

My greatest fear: "Of ever becoming a grown-up, please."

What is your idea of perfect happiness?
To see the children of the world receive their God-given rights. As Tolstoy said, "I shall not eat my piece of bread until everyone has a piece of their own." No one should starve while we eat.

What is your greatest fear?
Of ever becoming a grown-up, please.

Which historical figure do you most identify with?
John Johnson, Gordon Parks, Count Basie, and Duke Ellington.

What is your greatest extravagance?
Passion, love, and affection.

What do you consider the most overrated virtue?
Abstinence.

What do you dislike most about your appearance?
After I lose 16 pounds, I will have no dislikes whatsoever.

Which words or phrases do you most overuse?
"Can I have a little bit more of that?"

What is your greatest regret?
Since the age of 13, concentrating on arranging, orchestrating, and conducting instead of more songwriting, but it isn't too late.

What or who is the greatest love of your life?
My children, their children, my family, and my real friends.

When and where were you happiest?
Conducting and arranging for Frank Sinatra and Count Basie's band at the age of 31.

Which talent would you most like to have?
To be a great father.

What is your current state of mind?
Concern for the state of the world, and the joy of jiggling the molecules.

If you could change one thing about yourself, what would it be?
Not a damn thing. It is what it is.

What do you consider your greatest achievement?
My precious children. Each and every one of them.

If you could choose what to come back as, what would it be?
One of my daughters' dogs.

What do you regard as the lowest depth of misery?
When you are not able to turn darkness into light. It is a choice.

What is your favorite occupation?
Any form of creation from the blank page to the execution of a passion-driven vision.

What is your most marked characteristic?
Obsessive curiosity, a *joie de vivre,* and hugging.

What is the quality you most like in a man?
The ability to accept the female side in all of us.

What is the quality you most like in a woman?
An honest heart, a big mind, and inner and outer beauty.

Who are your favorite writers?
Aleksandr Pushkin, Ralph Ellison, Alice Walker, Maya Angelou, Pablo Neruda, and Toni Morrison.

Who is your favorite hero of fiction?
Pushkin's Eugene Onegin.

Who are your heroes in real life?
Nelson Mandela, Paul Kagame, Oprah Winfrey, Bill and Hillary Clinton, Barack Obama, Colin Powell, Sidney Poitier, Bono, Hani Masri, and the late Steve Ross.

What is it that you most dislike?
Bullshit!!!

How would you like to die?
In 2043, in my sleep, after working all day, having wine and dinner with my family and closest friends, and making passionate love with my lady. Not a second before.

What is your motto?
"I'd rather say, 'I'm sorry I did it,' than 'I wish I had,'" and "Live each day like it's the last, and do each task like it's the first."

July 2007

DONNA KARAN

FASHION DESIGNER

My favorite occupation: "Creating something from nothing."

What is your idea of perfect happiness?
Time off—no deadlines.

Which historical figure do you most identify with?
Isadora Duncan.

Which living person do you most admire?
The Dalai Lama.

What is the trait you most deplore in others?
Laziness.

What is your greatest extravagance?
Private planes.

What do you consider the most overrated virtue?
Beauty and patience.

What do you dislike most about your appearance?
My hips and aging face.

Which living person do you most despise?
I do not despise anyone.

What is your greatest regret?
Not spending enough time with my family.

What or who is the greatest love of your life?
My husband and children.

When and where were you happiest?
The day I met Steve and the day Gabby was born.

What do you consider your greatest achievement?
To continue to grow personally and professionally.

What is your most treasured possession?
My family, my photos, and my creative desire.

What do you regard as the lowest depth of misery?
My husband's death.

What is your favorite occupation?
Creating something from nothing.

What is your most marked characteristic?
Passion.

What is the quality you most like in a man?
His body and soul.

What is the quality you most like in a woman?
Warmth and aliveness.

Who is your favorite hero of fiction?
E.T.

Who are your heroes in real life?
Oprah, Hillary Clinton, Liz Tilberis, my husband,
the Dalai Lama, and Mother Teresa.

What are your favorite names?
Gabrielle.

What is it that you most dislike?
Boredom.

How would you like to die?
In the arms of someone I love.

What is your motto?
"Create something to make a difference
in this world."

May 2002

My real-life heroes: "My brothers."

Which historical figure do you most identify with?
My brothers Jack and Bobby.

Which living person do you most admire?
My wife, Vicki, because of all she does.

What is the trait you most deplore in yourself?
I gain weight just by looking at food.

What is the trait you most deplore in others?
Bigotry.

What is your greatest fear?
Another two years of Republican control of Congress.

What is your greatest extravagance?
Maintaining my 60-year-old wooden sailboat, *Mya*.

What is your idea of perfect happiness?
Sailing on *Mya* with Vicki at my side and my dogs, Splash and Sunny, at my feet. And, of course, a Democrat in the White House and regaining our majority in the Senate.

What is your favorite journey?
Driving down Route 6 on my way home to Hyannis Port.

What do you consider the most overrated virtue?
Silence.

On what occasion do you lie?
When I tell each of my sisters that she's the prettiest of them all.

What do you dislike most about your appearance?
I can't quite perfect that *GQ* crisp look.

Which living person do you most despise?
Osama bin Laden.

When and where were you happiest?
Every Thanksgiving, when our family gathers on Cape Cod.

Which talent would you most like to have?
Persuading more senators to vote as I do.

If you could change one thing about yourself, what would it be?
I'd have won in 1980.

If you could change one thing about your family, what would it be?
Jack would have had a second term.

What do you consider your greatest achievement?
Having children who turned out to be the loving, involved, and interesting people they are.

If you were to die and come back as a person or thing, what do you think it would be?
Probably a punching bag.

If you could choose what to come back as, what would it be?
One of the Three Tenors.

What is your most treasured possession?
My brother's dog tags from PT 109.

What do you regard as the lowest depth of misery?
Suddenly losing a loved one.

What is your favorite occupation?
U.S. senator.

What is your most marked characteristic?
Loyalty to friends and never giving up.

Who are your favorite writers?
Mark Twain, Seamus Heaney, and Doris Kearns Goodwin.

Who is your favorite hero of fiction?
James Bond.

Who are your heroes in real life?
My brothers.

What is it that you most dislike?
Poverty in this land of plenty.

What is your motto?
"The dream shall never die."

May 2006

EDWARD M. KENNEDY

MASSACHUSETTS SENATOR

LARRY KING

TALK-SHOW HOST

Which words or phrases do you most overuse?
"This will not be dull!" "Tune in tomorrow!"
"Only in America!"

What is your favorite occupation?
Exactly what I'm doing. I have the best job in my industry.

What is your idea of perfect happiness?
A smiling, happy, contented daughter.

When and where were you happiest?
The night my daughter, Chaia, was born—December 21,
1967, in Miami, Florida. It blew my mind.

What is your greatest fear?
Death. Having had a heart attack—trust me, this is a
big fear. I saw no lights, no angels—nothing.

What do you consider the most overrated virtue?
Patience—life is too short.

What is the trait you most deplore in yourself?
My inability to say no, which can lead to
three different lunches with three different people at
three different places on the same day.

What is the trait you most deplore in others?
Tardiness.

What is your greatest extravagance?
Ties and shirts and braces. A guy can't have too many.

What do you dislike most about your appearance?
My nose—for obvious reasons.
I would never have plastic surgery.

Which historical figure do you most identify with?
Lincoln. I abhor intolerance.

Which living person do you most despise?
David Duke and the Klan.

Who are your heroes in real life?
Stan Musial, Jackie Robinson, Adlai Stevenson.

What is the quality you most like in a man?
Loyalty.

What is the quality you most like in a woman?
Loyalty, intelligence, and pretty legs.

What is it that you most dislike?
Eggs—I hate the smell and look of them.

**If you were to die and come back as a person or thing,
what do you think it would be?**
Tommy Lasorda, [former] manager of the Dodgers.

**If you could choose what to come back as,
what would it be?**
Al Pacino. It would be nice to be Italian and have great
talent as an actor.

How would you like to die?
At age 106, in the arms of a 38-year-old Sharon Stone
look-alike, while in a deep sleep.

What is your motto?
"If at first you don't succeed, punt."

June 1995

"Having had a heart attack, [I] fear [death]. I saw no lights, no angels—nothing."

I most dislike:
"Monday mornings ..."

What is your idea of perfect happiness?
I am perfectly happy as long as I don't ask
myself if I am happy...

What is your greatest fear?
To lose my health. A boring subject, but life is more fun
when you feel great...

What is the trait you most deplore in yourself?
I got used to even my bad traits. Indifference is one of
them... I still fight against it.

What is the trait you most deplore in others?
I take people the way they are... with me... but that may
be also a part of my indifference.

What do you consider the most overrated virtue?
Manipulative religious hypocrisy.

On what occasion do you lie?
When it makes circumstances easier...

What do you dislike most about your appearance?
I spend my life working on that subject...

What is your greatest regret?
I have little regret for wrongdoings of my past.
Just a little remorse sometimes...

What or who is the greatest love of your life?
My life is not over yet. There is no other way to answer
such a question...

What is your current state of mind?
Much more positive than I expected it to be at my age...

What do you consider your greatest achievement?
It may sound strange: myself, or what I did with myself—
how I manipulated myself.

What is your most treasured possession?
I fight against possessions. They victimize you... if not,
little worthless things I would not mention.

What do you regard as the lowest depth of misery?
Ill health, unwanted loneliness, and—to be honest—
to be poor; or the three together...

Where would you like to live?
New York could be the next step... but I am not a
one-place person.

What is your favorite occupation?
My jobs: fashion, photography, publishing books. If not,
time with my friends and daydreaming.

What do you most value in your friends?
I take them as they are. Family you get—friends you have
to find ... Up to you to find the right friends without
too much questioning.

Who are your favorite writers?
In what language? I like poets best, E. Dickinson
(English), R. M. Rilke (German), Mallarmé (French),
Leopardi (Italian). I speak no other languages and I don't
believe in translated poetry...

Who is your favorite hero of fiction?
Virginia Woolf's Orlando...

Who are your heroes in real life?
There are a few, but I cannot mention them. Some
people would be surprised not to be on
the list—and others would be ... perhaps ...

What are your favorite names?
Tancrede (for boys), Allegra (for girls).

What is it that you most dislike?
Monday mornings...

How would you like to die?
I hate the idea of death—I prefer to
disappear...

September 2005

KARL LAGERFELD

FASHION DESIGNER

H E D Y L A M A R R

ACTRESS

The time and place I was happiest: "Between marriages."

What is your current state of mind?
Terrific.

What is your idea of perfect happiness?
Living a very private life.

What is your favorite occupation?
Playing poker.

What is your most treasured possession?
My sense of humor.

What is your greatest fear?
Being stuck in a crowd.

What is your favorite journey?
Exploring life.

What is your greatest extravagance?
For instance, at a party, Gertrude Lawrence admired my 20-carat star-sapphire ring, so I gave it to her.

On what occasion do you lie?
When I am tired of standing.

Which words or phrases do you most overuse?
"Oh, my God!" and "basically."

What or who is the greatest love of your life?
My father.

What do you consider your greatest achievement?
Having been a parent.

When and where were you happiest?
Between marriages.

If you could change one thing about yourself, what would it be?
My nail polish.

What is it that you most dislike?
Snobbery.

Which historical figure do you most identify with?
Empress Elizabeth of Austria.

Which living person do you most admire?
Michael Tilson Thomas, the conductor.

Who are your favorite writers?
Kahlil Gibran and Tennessee Williams.

Who is your favorite hero of fiction?
Bart Simpson.

Who are your heroes in real life?
Franklin Roosevelt and Winston Churchill.

How would you like to die?
Preferably after sex.

If you were to die and come back as a person or thing, what do you think it would be?
An owl.

If you could choose what to come back as, what would it be?
An owl.

What is your motto?
"Do not take things too seriously."

April 1999
(Lamarr died in 2000.)

ELEANOR LAMBERT

FASHION ARBITER

The trait I most deplore: "Egocentricity."

What is the quality you like most in a person?
Charm. The Queen Mother was one of the most charming people I've known. And Eleanor Roosevelt was certainly charming. Of people I know today, Sister Parish is always the most charming because she's just herself and has so much knowledge and a sense of beauty. The most charming man I know today is Mark Birley, who owns Annabel's.

What is your idea of perfect happiness?
A good and lasting marriage with whatever ups and downs might come along.

Which talent would you most like to have?
Eloquence.

What is the trait you most deplore in others?
Egocentricity. It has destroyed many people, like Salvador Dalí.

What is your most treasured possession?
It's so corny to say it—my wedding ring. I still have it on and I've never taken it off since I was married in 1936.

What is your greatest extravagance?
Blackamoor jewelry, old porcelain, and lush bed linens. I'm an old-linen person. I have some that were given to me that belonged to one of the Astor ladies from the turn of the century.

On what occasion do you lie?
Not enough.

What is your favorite journey?
To food or flea markets. As far as restaurants go, I like places that aren't noted only for excellent food but also for having wonderful people around: Le Cirque, Harry's Bar in London, Lespinasse.

What do you dislike most about your appearance?
Problem hair. The waif look is coming back, but not for me.

When and where were you happiest?
I've been happy a great deal of my life. I love seeing things start up that are exciting and have a future, whether it's a career or a project or a new building. Some of the great talents I've watched and shared in promoting were Liza Minnelli and Donna Karan, and both are in the spotlight now.

What is your most marked characteristic?
My curiosity.

Who is your favorite hero of fiction?
Sherlock Holmes. Goes with the curiosity.

What do you regard as the lowest depth of misery?
Having nothing to read.

Who are your favorite writers?
Freya Stark, Lesley Blanch, Josephine Tey, Bill Berkson, Agatha Christie, Art Buchwald, M. F. K. Fisher, Winston Churchill, Cecil Beaton, and Aileen Mehle (Suzy).

What do you most value in your friends?
The pleasure of their company.

If you were to die and come back as a person or thing, what do you think it would be?
I can't think of anybody that I'd want to come back as. We've all gone through that thing of talking with somebody who tells you who you were in a previous life. I've been everything from a Chinese peasant to a vestal virgin to a queen.

If you could choose what to come back as, what would it be?
I'd like to come back as an interesting person and as a woman.

What is your motto?
"Never look back."

January 1994
(Lambert died in 2003.)

TIMOTHY LEARY

COUNTERCULTURE PIONEER

My motto: "Dial On, Tune In, Hang Out, Link Up, Escape-Delete."

What do you consider your greatest achievement?
Joyfully engineering and channeling and surfing the last four Cultural Revolutions (Jazz, Acid, Punk, Cyber-Tech).

Which talent would you most like to have?
More time, more time. To learn to play the blues.

What is your most marked characteristic?
Aesthetically precise, arrogant Communicator.

What is your favorite occupation?
Babbling and goofing with smart, silly aesthetic pals.

What do you consider the most overrated virtue?
All virtues are overrated.

Which words or phrases do you most overuse?
I, Me, Chaos, Fuck, Me, Interactive, Memory Loss, Victimhood, Fuck, Well, let's talk about this later.

What or who is the greatest love of your life?
My wife (at the time).

Which living person do you most admire?
Yoko Ono, so far.

Which living person do you most despise?
Me! Myself! Me! Hey, I spend around 10 minutes every morning in bed reviewing the despicable misdeeds committed yesterday. "[You] didn't listen." "[You] talked too much." "[You were] boorish, arrogant, self-indulgent." "Just a Senile Sunset Stripper, a Geriatric Party Animal. A fringe celebrity in this bizarre village of stellar talent."

Which historical figure do you most identify with?
Socrates, Voltaire, Ralph Waldo Emerson, Henry David Thoreau, Yoko Ono.

Who is your favorite hero of fiction?
Huck Finn, Susan Sarandon, and me. So far.

Who are your heroes in real life?
Prometheus, Thomas Edison, Barbara Fouch, John Roseboro, Marshall McLuhan, Margaret Fuller, Susan Sarandon, and Yoko Ono. So far.

Who are your favorite writers?
Mark Twain, Voltaire, Brenda Laurel, James Joyce, Thomas Pynchon, Gertrude Stein, William Gibson, Yoko Ono, and me.

How would you like to die?
At the moment when my Quality of Life Index falls below the tolerable. I plan to De-Animate—i.e., to snuff my body. Me and my friends are planning the happiest, joyable, organically sensitive Dying Celebrations in human history. The preparations for my Sui-Cide have already begun. Every stage in the process is being filmed and some of it will be broadcast on the World Wide Web. I hope that millions of people will be online during the last stages of my celebratory good-bye party.

If you were to die and come back as a person or thing, what do you think it would be?
A beautiful, smart, brave, funny Asian woman.

If you could choose what to come back as, what would it be?
Me, as a hip 21st-century media wizard. With Her, of course.

What is your motto?
"Dial On, Tune In, Hang Out, Link Up, Escape-Delete."

June 1996
(Leary died in May 1996, around the time this questionnaire was first published.)

FRAN LEBOWITZ

WRITER, HUMORIST, *and* SOCIAL CRITIC

How I would like to die: "Vindicated."

What is your idea of perfect happiness?
Silence.

What is your greatest fear?
Noise.

What is the trait you most deplore in yourself?
Sloth.

What is the trait you most deplore in others?
Industry.

What is your greatest extravagance?
Thrift.

What do you consider the most overrated virtue?
Abstinence.

On what occasion do you lie?
Before.

What do you dislike most about your appearance?
After.

What is your current state of mind?
Warranted.

If you could change one thing about your family, what would it be?
Passover.

What do you consider your greatest achievement?
Restraint.

If you were to die and come back as a person or thing, what do you think it would be?
Thing.

What is your most treasured possession?
English.

What do you regard as the lowest depth of misery?
French.

What is your favorite occupation?
Pope.

Where would you like to live?
Rome.

What is your most marked characteristic?
Optimism.

What is the quality you most like in a man?
Height.

What is the quality you most like in a woman?
Depth.

Who is your favorite hero of fiction?
Truth.

Who is your hero in real life?
Consequence.

What is your favorite name?
Driver.

What do you most value in your friends?
Typing.

How would you like to die?
Vindicated.

November 1994

The occasion when I lie: "Just give me a chance."

What is your idea of perfect happiness?
Being with my entire family while I'm filming a hit picture or doing a play.

Which historical figure do you most identify with?
Maxie Kuhnfartz (former agent who operated out of a phone booth).

Which living person do you most admire?
Nelson Mandela.

What is the trait you most deplore in yourself?
Promptness.

What is your greatest extravagance?
Buying automobiles. (I'm a complete car nut.)

What is your favorite journey?
Going fishing with my son in Alaska each September (catch and release, by all means).

On what occasion do you lie?
Just give me a chance.

Which living person do you most despise?
A critic at the *Long Island Bullet*.

What or who is the greatest love of your life?
My wife, Felicia.

When and where were you happiest?
When we were married in Paris 100 years ago.

Which talent would you most like to have?
George Gershwin's.

What is your current state of mind?
I can't wait until this is over. I would be playing golf instead of doing this.

What do you consider your greatest achievement?
I am not sure it's an achievement rather than the luck of the draw, but my wife, our children, and our grandchildren.

If you were to die and come back as a person or thing, what do you think it would be?
A standard poodle, like my Chloe.

What is your most treasured possession?
My family.

What do you regard as the lowest depth of misery?
Since I have been fortunate in my life, my lowest depth of misery is missing a one-foot putt on the 18th hole.

What is your favorite occupation?
Acting, composing, and golfing.

What is the quality you most like in a man?
Generosity, compassion, and a sense of humor.

What is the quality you most like in a woman?
Imitating that man.

Who are your favorite writers?
Shakespeare, O'Neill, Peter Matthiessen.

What is your motto?
"Magic time."

October 2000
(Lemmon died in 2001.)

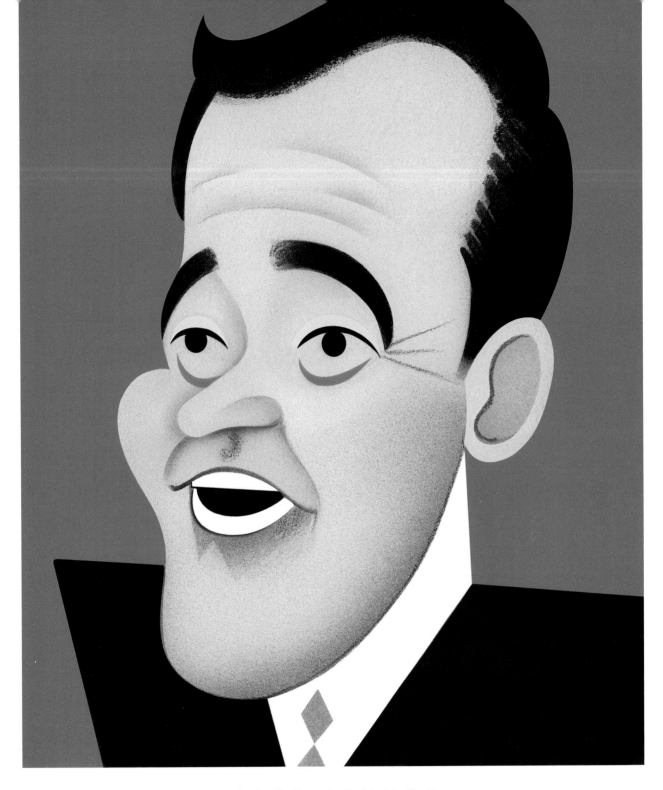

JACK LEMMON

ACTOR

LITTLE RICHARD

MUSICIAN

"My greatest achievement was finding God."

What is your idea of perfect happiness?
Being at peace with God.

What is your greatest fear?
I don't want to be lost and burn in hell.

What is the trait you most deplore in others?
Selfishness—people who don't care about others or their feelings and will do or say anything as long as they get what they want.

What is your greatest extravagance?
I realize that some people don't have any way to make a living and I feel obligated to help them. As long as God gives me the strength to go on and perform and make a decent living, I'll go on helping the people around me.

What do you dislike most about your appearance?
At this stage in my life I just wish I were younger.

What is your greatest regret?
That I didn't move to the country when I was younger. When I became famous, I moved to Los Angeles and brought my family with me. But I love to see the seasons change—like on the East Coast—and wish I had moved back there years ago.

When and where were you happiest?
In Macon, Georgia, during my childhood. I knew everybody there—it was like the whole town was your family. I felt complete there.

Which talent would you most like to have?
The talent to be a minister.

If you could change one thing about yourself, what would it be?
To be taller. I've been looking up at certain people all my life. If I was taller, I could look down and see them a lot better.

What do you consider your greatest achievement?
My greatest achievement was finding God. After that is my fame.

If you could choose what to come back as, what would it be?
I would still come back as me—born into the same family all over again.

What is your most treasured possession?
The Word of God: the Bible.

What do you most value in your friends?
Unselfishness. I like to surround myself with people who are kind and have feelings for others and their problems.

What is your motto?
"Do unto others as you would have them do unto you."

November 2001

My greatest fear: "The violence of enlightenment."

What is your idea of perfect happiness?
Searching for it.

What is your greatest fear?
The violence of enlightenment.

Which living person do you most admire?
The people who work with and for me.

What is the trait you most deplore in yourself?
My impatience, which can cause me to be really caustic and rude.

What is the trait you most deplore in others?
Same. We detest in others what we detest in ourselves.

What do you consider the most overrated virtue?
Monogamy.

On what occasion do you lie?
When I eat sugar and say it doesn't matter.

What do you dislike most about your appearance?
My bloated stomach after eating sugar.

What is your greatest regret?
Not spending more time with my daughter when I was working.

What or who is the greatest love of your life?
My dog Terry. All of nature.

Which talent would you most like to have?
Being patient with people who have no work ethic. Maybe they have something to teach me.

What is your current state of mind?
Content, but discontent with the leadership worldwide.

If you could change one thing about yourself, what would it be?
Being able to do nothing.

What do you consider your greatest achievement?
The way I think.

If you were to die and come back as a person or thing, what do you think it would be?
A zillionaire who gives away all his money. Yes, I would like to come back as a rich *man* who would live without corruption, respect nature, women, and small, insignificant things.

What is your most treasured possession?
Two necklaces from my Camino de Santiago de Compostela. All of my animals.

What do you regard as the lowest depth of misery?
Prison.

Where would you like to live?
Wherever I am with Terry, but not in a confined space. New Mexico is fine for me.

What is your most marked characteristic?
My humorous cynicism.

Who are your favorite writers?
Those who tell the truth about themselves.

Who is your favorite hero of fiction?
I don't read fiction. My life is fiction.

Who are your heroes in real life?
Those who are optimistic through pain. I am a physical pussy unless I'm dancing or working out.

What is it that you most dislike?
People who don't care about themselves.

What is your motto?
"I am part of God in Light."

November 2007

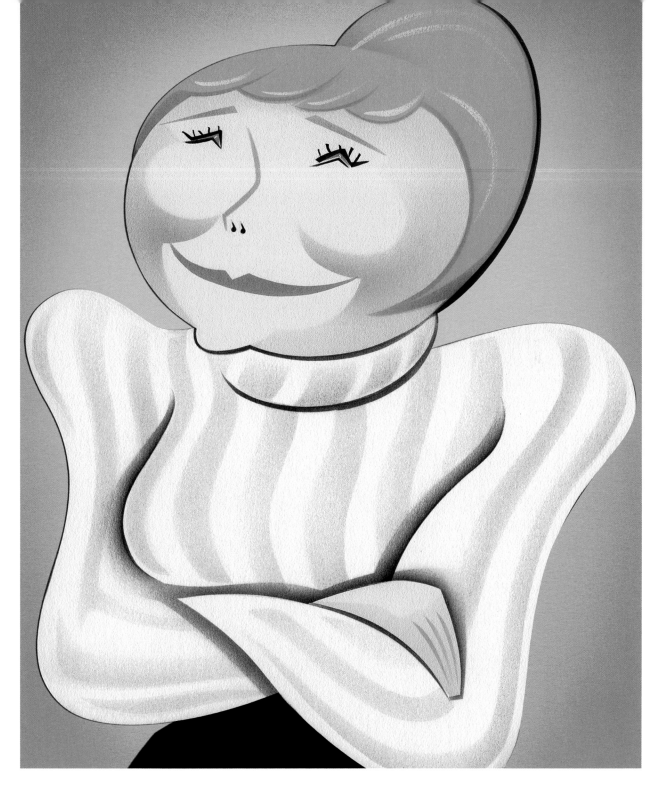

SHIRLEY MacLAINE

ACTRESS

NORMAN MAILER

WRITER

I most identify with: "Hemingway. His suicide suggested the unseen perils of my profession."

What is your idea of perfect happiness?
Let the next 35 responses offer their clues. A fool draws a road map to his magic city.

What is your greatest fear?
That I will never meet [*New York Times* reviewer] Michiko Kakutani and so not be able to tell her what I think of her. She has an unseemly haste to rush into print with the first very bad review of any book I write. She does this ahead of publication. That is a strategy. If the first review of a book is dreadful, an author needs at least three good ones to change that first impression.

Which historical figure do you most identify with?
Hemingway. His suicide suggested the unseen perils of my profession.

Which living person do you most admire?
Muhammad Ali.

What is the trait you most deplore in yourself?
Inanition—it comes on me from time to time. I also detest it in others. A judge will never forgive a criminal for a crime he is capable of committing himself.

What is the trait you most deplore in others?
Banality. For that matter, it's a close cousin to inanition.

What is your greatest extravagance?
Restaurants.

What is your favorite journey?
It used to be crossing the Brooklyn Bridge when homeward bound from a good dinner in Manhattan. Now it's the sight of Provincetown as one rides up over the last rise and there is the Pilgrim Monument in all its subtle presence.

What do you consider the most overrated virtue?
Prayer. Of all the lofty practices, it is the most abused. Church professionals lead the scurry crew who profit from pushing prayer.

On what occasion do you lie?
Most of all when playing Texas Hold 'Em.

What do you dislike most about your appearance?
Forgive me. I'll skip this laundry list.

Which living person do you most despise?
Well, it used to be Ronald Reagan. He was the most ignorant president we ever had. Now George W. has appropriated his seat.

CONTINUED ON PAGE 132 >

NORMAN MAILER

WRITER

‹ CONTINUED FROM PAGE 131

Which words or phrases do you most overuse?
It is not easy to construct a complex sentence without using "that."

What is your greatest regret?
The memory of the books I promised to write and didn't.

What or who is the greatest love of your life?
Norris Church Mailer, my wife of these last 30 years.

Which talent would you most like to have?
There are several kinds of athletes I wouldn't have minded becoming. There is also the ability to sing. I once described my voice in the following manner: "Mailer vocalizes with the matchless authority of a man who has never been known to hit a note on pitch."

What is your current state of mind?
Benevolent—astonishingly so. It's one of the few perks of old age when it's there.

If you could change one thing about your family, what would it be?
Hey, they're perfect.

What do you consider your greatest achievement?
I look to entertain the notion that it is to be found in my latest novel.

If you were to die and come back as a person or thing, what do you think it would be?
What an idiocy! God, if He or She is paying any attention, would have a wittier notion of how to punish and reward the first stages of one's new existence.

If you could choose what to come back as, what would it be?
I would like to be a novelist who is more accomplished than the last one.

What is your most treasured possession?
I am just superstitious enough not to name it.

What do you regard as the lowest depth of misery?
Wasting my days.

Where would you like to live?
Where I have lived—Brooklyn Heights years ago and now in Provincetown. Until you get to Maine there is no more beautiful town on the Eastern Seaboard of the U.S.

What is your favorite occupation?
One always returns to writing. I resist the temptation to say that good fucking is really my favorite. One is now too old to talk like that.

The quality I most like in a man: "There to stand up when called."

What is your most marked characteristic?
I'd like to think that I know how to push the envelope. It's become a necessary virtue. We Americans have become so uneasy, so stupid, so guilty, and so flatulently patriotic that we are in danger of ruining a fine land.

What is the quality you most like in a man?
There to stand up when called.

What is the quality you most like in a woman?
Beauty, mystery, wit, and the inner superiority to be above political correctness.

What do you most value in your friends?
Loyalty, wit, and, believe it or not, the power to come forth with close criticism.

Who are your favorite writers?
I'll only mention the dead. Every live author you do not mention will never forgive you. So, I'll list Tolstoy, Dostoyevsky, Chekhov, Stendhal, Melville, Hemingway, Faulkner, Dos Passos, Proust, Zola, Mann, Goethe, and, oh yes—curses—Shakespeare!

Who is your favorite hero of fiction?
Let's say not the hero but the protagonist from whom I learned the most. That might be Anna Karenina.

Who are your heroes in real life?
So few. F.D.R., J.F.K. Also, de Gaulle and Castro; yes, one must put up with the worst of these two, but they were heroic in their day. Heroism may be of greater value to civilization than political achievement.

What are your favorite names?
I have nine children. I would list their names.

What is it that you most dislike?
Overweening piety used for political purposes. Hitler and Himmler come to mind. So do a few minor American figures in high places today.

How would you like to die?
Without undue fear—which is to say die with the same confidence I have now that there is another world one enters, and so the finest of all the clichés is that death is a great adventure.

What is your motto?
That should be obvious. It has to be "Excelsior!" [Onward and upward.]

January 2007
(Mailer died in November 2007.)

DAVID MAMET

PLAYWRIGHT *and* DIRECTOR

"My idea of perfect happiness [is that] all the critics die."

What is your idea of perfect happiness?
My idea of perfect happiness is a healthy family, peace between nations, and all the critics die.

What is your greatest fear?
My greatest fear is that the audience will beat me to the punch line.

What is your greatest extravagance?
My greatest extravagance was, on moving house in Boston, empowering my decorator to conduct the whole procedure while I was away on location.

What do you regard as the lowest depth of misery?
My lowest depth of misery was, on my return, the discovery that she had moved me into the wrong house.

What is the quality you most like in a man?
The quality I most admire in a man is steadfastness.

What is the quality you most like in a woman?
The quality I most admire in a woman is kindness. And that they should look good in blue jeans.

What or who is the greatest love of your life?
The greatest love of my life is my wife and my kids.

Which talent would you most like to have?
The talent I would most like to have is the ability to cloud men's minds. This was possessed by Lamont Cranston (The Shadow [of the 1930s radio show]) and various East European stage directors.

What do you consider your greatest achievement?
I consider my greatest achievement the few times I have refrained from telling various producers to go fuck themselves.

If you were to die and come back as a person or thing, what do you think it would be?
If I were to die and come back as a person or thing, it would be a person.

What is your favorite occupation?
My favorite occupation is directing a movie. This beats napping—not by much, but nonetheless.

What is your most treasured possession?
My most treasured possession is the urn containing the ashes of my dog Fluff. There is not much difference between contemplating the urn and looking at my *current* dog, asleep on the couch. But I do not have to walk the urn.

What is your most marked characteristic?
My most marked characteristic is an all-inclusive, nonjudgmental joy in the constantly diverting multiplicity of human beings. And foreigners.

What do you most value in your friends?
What I value most in my friends is loyalty.

Who are your favorite writers?
My favorite writers are Theodore Dreiser, Willa Cather, Dawn Powell, George V. Higgins, Patrick O'Brian, and John le Carré.

Who are your heroes in real life?
My heroes in real life are firemen.

What is your greatest regret?
My greatest regret is that I was never a fireman.

How would you like to die?
I would not like to die.

What is your motto?
My motto is "Be Prepared." I am told this is also the motto of the Boy Scouts, but, if so, this only proves that they were *acting according to my motto* earlier than I.

May 2008

What is your greatest fear?
Filling out questionnaires.

What is your current state of mind?
Excellent.

What is your favorite occupation?
Acting.

Which historical figure do you most identify with?
Jack the Ripper.

Which living person do you most admire?
Madonna.

Who is your favorite hero of fiction?
Tarzan.

Who are your heroes in real life?
My wife.

What is your most treasured possession?
My wife.

When and where were you happiest?
In bed with my wife.

What is your most marked characteristic?
My decency.

What is the trait you most deplore in yourself?
Decency.

What is the trait you most deplore in others?
Decency.

What is your greatest extravagance?
Sweaters.

What is your favorite journey?
To the kitchen.

What do you dislike most about your appearance?
My ties.

What do you consider the most overrated virtue?
Honesty.

On what occasion do you lie?
On any occasion.

Which words or phrases do you most overuse?
"You know."

If you could change one thing about yourself, what would it be?
My posture.

What do you consider your greatest achievement?
Getting out of high school.

Where would you like to live?
Near the ocean.

What is the quality you most like in a man?
Honesty.

What is the quality you most like in a woman?
Deception.

What is it that you most dislike?
Honesty.

What do you most value in your friends?
Their ability to pay their debts.

How would you like to die?
I wouldn't like it.

If you were to die and come back as a person or thing, what do you think it would be?
A good book.

If you could choose what to come back as, what would it be?
A Siberian tiger.

What is your motto?
"Fuck you."

April 1997
(Matthau died in 2000.)

I most value in my friends:
"Their ability to pay their debts."

WALTER MATTHAU

ACTOR

ELAINE MAY

COMEDIAN, WRITER, *and* FILMMAKER

My motto: "Don't throw away designer clothes."

What is your idea of perfect happiness?
Healthy junk food.

What is your greatest fear?
Forgetting the punch line of a joke while
I'm telling it, and/or death.

What is the trait you most deplore in others?
Cocky ignorance.

What is the trait you most deplore in yourself?
Fortunately I've conquered it.

What is your greatest extravagance?
Wasting time.

What is your current state of mind?
Fraught.

What do you consider the most overrated virtue?
Virtue.

On what occasion do you lie?
When answering questionnaires.

What is the quality you most like in a man?
Generosity.

What is the quality you most like in a woman?
Patience. Oddly, it's a quality none of
the women that I like have.

If you were to die and come back as a person or thing, what do you think it would be?
The only child of two genetically perfect billionaires.

Which words or phrases do you most overuse?
"You're kidding" and "Oh, fuck" and
"Oh, fuck, you're kidding."

What or who is the greatest love of your life?
My daughter.

When and where were you happiest?
Thursday, 3:15, 1998, Bowdle, South Dakota.

What do you consider your greatest achievement?
I'm hoping I haven't achieved it yet.

Where would you like to live?
On a train.

What do you regard as the lowest depth of misery?
Bad X-rays.

What is your most marked characteristic?
My breasts. Or do you mean something else?

What do you most value in your friends?
Availability. Just kidding. Character.

Who are your favorite writers?
A lot of the Russians, a lot of the French,
Jane Austen, Rex Stout.

Who are your heroes in real life?
Oskar Schindler, Miep Gies, Doctors Without Borders—
that whole crowd.

What is your greatest regret?
Having a time limit.

What is your motto?
"Don't throw away designer clothes."

How would you like to die?
I've given that question a lot of thought.
There is no way I would like to die.

March 2009

SUE MENGERS

HOLLYWOOD AGENT

The living person I most admire: "My plumber."

What is your idea of perfect happiness?
To be left alone.

What is your greatest fear?
Insects.

Which historical figure do you most identify with?
Golda Meir.

Which living person do you most admire?
My plumber.

What is the trait you most deplore in yourself?
There's not enough paper . . .

What is the trait you most deplore in others?
Lack of humor.

What is your greatest extravagance?
Grass.

What is your favorite journey?
From the living room to the bedroom.

On what occasion do you lie?
In order not to hurt someone.

What do you dislike most about your appearance?
My height, or, rather, lack of it.

Which words or phrases do you most overuse?
"O.K., next," "When I was alive," and "HellOHH!"

What is your greatest regret?
That I never represented Fatty Arbuckle.

What or who is the greatest love of your life?
Jean-Claude Tramont.

When and where were you happiest?
Anytime in Ravello with Jean-Claude.

Which talent would you most like to have?
I'd take any one.

If you could change one thing about your family, what would it be?
That I don't have any.

What do you consider your greatest achievement?
Not having children.

If you were to die and come back as a person or thing, what do you think it would be?
A pussycat.

If you could choose what to come back as, what would it be?
Paris Hilton.

What is your most treasured possession?
My sense of humor and my bed.

What is your favorite occupation?
Sleeping.

What is your most marked characteristic?
My weight.

What is the quality you most like in a man?
That he breathes.

What is the quality you most like in a woman?
Forgiveness.

What do you most value in your friends?
Utter devotion.

Who are your heroes in real life?
Doctors.

What is it that you most dislike?
A leaking roof.

How would you like to die?
I think I already have.

What is your motto?
"Tomorrow may *not* be another day."

June 2005

What is your idea of perfect happiness?
An empty house and a good book.

What is your greatest fear?
That the greatest days of my country are past.

What is the trait you most deplore in yourself?
Impatience.

What is the trait you most deplore in others?
Ignorance and arrogance.

What is your greatest extravagance?
Flowers and philanthropy.

What is your current state of mind?
Agitated.

On what occasion do you lie?
Who needs an occasion?

What do you dislike most about your appearance?
My roots.

Which living person do you most despise?
The Bluetooth-wearing S.U.V. driver who idles in front of my building.

What is the quality you most like in a man?
Guts.

What is the quality you most like in a woman?
Balls.

Which words or phrases do you most overuse?
"I gotta get crackin'."

Which talent would you most like to have?
The ability to read a spreadsheet.

What do you consider your greatest achievement?
My daughter, Sophie.

If you were to die and come back as a person or thing, what do you think it would be?
The wind.

Where would you like to live?
At Sissinghurst.

What is your most treasured possession?
My sanity.

What do you most value in your friends?
A talent to amuse.

Who are your favorite writers?
Nabokov and P. G. Wodehouse.

Who is your favorite hero of fiction?
Ignatius J. Reilly.

Which historical figure do you most identify with?
Wallis Simpson and Johnny Appleseed.

What is it that you most dislike?
Pollution and polluters.

What is your motto?
"Fuck 'em if they can't take a joke."

August 2008

Who I most despise: "The Bluetooth-wearing S.U.V. driver who idles in front of my building."

BETTE MIDLER

ENTERTAINER, ACTRESS, *and* COMEDIAN

ARTHUR MILLER

PLAYWRIGHT

My greatest regret: "Not knowing at 30 what I knew about women at 60."

What is your idea of perfect happiness?
A good night's sleep.

What is your greatest fear?
Losing memory.

Which historical figure do you most identify with?
Lincoln.

What is the trait you most deplore in yourself?
Waning curiosity.

What is the trait you most deplore in others?
Self-satisfaction.

What is your greatest extravagance?
New York restaurants.

What is your favorite journey?
Angkor Wat to Thailand, to escape Nixon-Kissinger bombing.

On what occasion do you lie?
When pressed to reveal family matters; also when I forget to show up as agreed.

Which words or phrases do you most overuse?
I. Tremendous. Stupid. Idiot. Dream.

What is your greatest regret?
Not knowing at 30 what I knew about women at 60.

What or who is the greatest love of your life?
Ingeborg Morath. The *idea* of tragedy.

When and where were you happiest?
At home, when learning that the dying Eugene O'Neill said that *Death of a Salesman* was a great work.

If you could change one thing about your family, what would it be?
They're perfect.

What do you consider your greatest achievement?
That I can still muster up some hope for humans.

What is your most treasured possession?
The cherry dining table I made a long time ago.

What do you regard as the lowest depth of misery?
Betrayal.

Where would you like to live?
Connecticut and New York, as I do.

What is your favorite occupation?
Writing a funny line.

What is your most marked characteristic?
Utter modesty.

What is the quality you most like in a man?
Loyalty to his craft.

What is the quality you most like in a woman?
A warm welcome.

Who is your favorite hero of fiction?
The hero of *Catch-22*—Captain John Yossarian.

Who are your heroes in real life?
There are none in real life except a few firefighters, perhaps.

How would you like to die?
Quickly.

If you were to die and come back as a person or thing, what do you think it would be?
A tree, maybe a locust.

If you could choose what to come back as, what would it be?
A poet, naturally. Like Shakespeare, maybe.

What is your motto?
"Don't rush, it'll wait. Meanwhile, hurry!"

March 1999
(Miller died in 2005.)

WILLIE NELSON

MUSICIAN

The most overrated virtue: "Humility."

What is your idea of perfect happiness?
How I feel right now.

What is your greatest fear?
Fear.

Which historical figure do you most identify with?
Billy the Kid.

What is the trait you most deplore in yourself?
Stupidity.

What is the trait you most deplore in others?
Stupidity.

What is your favorite journey?
On the road, touring.

What do you consider the most overrated virtue?
Humility.

On what occasion do you lie?
I NEVER LIE!

When and where were you happiest?
Onstage.

If you could change one thing about your family, what would it be?
That they'd still all be here.

What do you consider your greatest achievement?
My music.

If you were to die and come back as a person or thing, what do you think it would be?
A snake.

What is your most treasured possession?
My guitar, Trigger.

What do you regard as the lowest depth of misery?
Self-pity.

Where would you like to live?
On the bus.

What is your most marked characteristic?
Stubbornness.

What is the quality you most like in a man?
Stubbornness.

What do you most value in your friends?
Honesty.

Who are your favorite writers?
Kris Kristofferson and Hank Williams.

Who is your favorite hero of fiction?
Superman.

Who are your heroes in real life?
Ray Charles, Merle Haggard, Kris Kristofferson, Hank Williams, and Ray Price, to name a few.

What are your favorite names?
Gene and Roy.

What is it that you most dislike?
Dishonesty.

What is your motto?
"Fortunately, we're not in control."

May 2003

PAUL NEWMAN

ACTOR *and* ACTIVIST

My greatest achievement:
"Being No. 19 on Nixon's enemies list."

What is your current state of mind?
Since I have a pulse, it's pretty optimistic.

What do you consider your greatest achievement?
Being No. 19 on Nixon's enemies list.

What is your most treasured possession?
The Proust Questionnaire.

What is your idea of perfect happiness?
Viagra for the brain.

What is your greatest fear?
Dinner with Rupert Murdoch.

What is your favorite journey?
From here to the beer cooler.

Which historical figure do you most identify with?
Achilles. Why? Because he was such a heel.

Which living person do you most admire?
Above the waist, Linda Tripp.
Below the waist, Lucianne Goldberg.

On what occasion do you lie?
Every chance I get.

Which words or phrases do you most overuse?
"Yes."

What or who is the greatest love of your life?
Dry heaves.

Which talent would you most like to have?
That of the great Formula One racecar driver Juan Fangio.

What is the trait you most deplore in yourself?
Having only two ties, one suit.

What is the trait you most deplore in others?
Having 40 ties, 60 suits.

What is your greatest extravagance?
Two ties.

What do you consider the most overrated virtue?
Stinginess.

What is the quality you most like in a man?
Two ties.

What is the quality you most like in a woman?
No ties.

What do you most value in your friends?
House seats.

If you were to die and come back as a person or thing, what do you think it would be?
Dust.

If you could choose what to come back as, what would it be?
Ditto.

January 1999
(Newman died in 2008.)

CONAN O'BRIEN

COMEDIAN *and* TALK-SHOW HOST

What is your idea of perfect happiness?
A long walk on the beach with my Israeli bodyguards.

What is your greatest fear?
Puberty.

Which historical figure do you most identify with?
Mrs. Herbert Hoover.

What is the trait you most deplore in yourself?
My inability to tan.

What is the trait you most deplore in others?
Their ability to tan.

What is your favorite journey?
Home, to my best girl, after winning World War II.

What do you consider the most overrated virtue?
Kindness to the less fortunate.

What do you dislike most about your appearance?
My penetrating blue eyes.

Which living person do you most despise?
Pat Robertson. But not that Pat Robertson.
The Pat Robertson who stole my bike.

Which words or phrases do you most overuse?
"Ditto." "You go, girl." "I'm the Pope, dammit."

What is your greatest regret?
Turning down the Samuel L. Jackson role
in *Pulp Fiction.*

Which talent would you most like to have?
The ability to make people laugh.

If you could change one thing about your family, what would it be?
Their blind devotion to Charles Manson.

What do you consider your greatest achievement?
My 12 beautiful children.

What is the quality you most like in a woman?
A lust for mediocrity.

What do you most value in your friends?
Their potential as eye donors.

Who are your favorite writers?
Flannery O'Connor, F. Scott Fitzgerald, Woody Allen.

What are your favorite names?
Cornelius, T-Bone, Jesus (pronounced "HAY-soos").

How would you like to die?
In a slo-mo shoot-out with Eli Wallach.

What is your motto?
"Ape must not kill ape."

June 2000

The quality I most like in a woman: "A lust for mediocrity."

If I were to die and come back, it would be as: "My enemy."

When and where were you happiest?
When the war was over—whichever war that was.

Which living person do you most admire?
Myself.

What is your most marked characteristic?
Modesty.

What is the trait you most deplore in yourself?
Modesty.

What is the trait you most deplore in others?
Arrogance.

What do you consider the most overrated virtue?
Modesty.

What is your favorite occupation?
Counting my virtues.

What is it that you most dislike?
Hypocrisy.

What is your greatest regret?
That I'm not tall, slim, and flat-chested.

What or who is the greatest love of your life?
Me—that is, if I were tall, skinny, and flat-chested.

Who is your favorite hero of fiction?
Me.

Who are your heroes in real life?
Me.

What are your favorite names?
John, Sean, and Kyoko.

Who are your favorite writers?
Me, me, me, and John—not necessarily in that order.

Which words or phrases do you most overuse?
"Me."

Which historical figure do you most identify with?
Arnold Schwarzenegger.

Which living person do you most despise?
I forgot.

Which talent would you most like to have?
I've got enough to handle.

What do you consider your greatest achievement?
Something I would achieve in the future.

What is the quality you most like in a man?
Being available.

What is the quality you most like in a woman?
Not being too mean to me.

If you were to die and come back as a person or thing, what do you think it would be?
My enemy.

How would you like to die?
In my sleep—smiling.

What is your motto?
"Keep smiling and maybe you'll get something to really smile about."

December 1995

YOKO ONO

ARTIST

BILL O'REILLY

POLITICAL COMMENTATOR *and* TALK-SHOW HOST

If I could change one thing, it would be: "My penchant for alienating people."

What is your idea of perfect happiness?
Seeing little kids having a great time.

What is your greatest fear?
Failure.

Which historical figure do you most identify with?
Robert Kennedy. My mother comes from the Kennedy clan, and R.F.K. had the fire of a reformer and the determination to get things done. He was one of the few politicians who actually got angry at social injustice.

What is the trait you most deplore in yourself?
I am impatient and intractable at times.

What is the trait you most deplore in others?
Cowardice.

What is your favorite journey?
Tahiti, especially Bora-Bora.

What do you consider the most overrated virtue?
Conformity—it destroys the creative spirit.

On what occasion do you lie?
To protect the feelings of others in trivial matters.

Which living person do you most despise?
Osama bin Laden.

What is your greatest regret?
That my father didn't live long enough to see his son take the fight to the bad guys. He would have loved the crusading aspect of *The O'Reilly Factor*.

Which talent would you most like to have?
The ability to sing like Jim Morrison.

If you could change one thing about yourself, what would it be?
My penchant for alienating people.

If you could choose what to come back as, what would it be?
President of the United States.

What is your most treasured possession?
My family—although I don't possess them. Worldly possessions don't much interest me.

What do you regard as the lowest depth of misery?
Drug addiction.

What is your most marked characteristic?
Irish temper, but it's not my fault. You can't fight genes.

What is the quality you most like in a man?
Sense of humor.

What is the quality you most like in a woman?
Sense of humor about sex.

Who are your favorite writers?
James Lee Burke, James M. McPherson, Washington Irving, Graham Greene, James Ellroy, Mario Puzo.

Who is your favorite hero of fiction?
"Dirty Harry" Callahan.

Who are your heroes in real life?
Jesus of Nazareth, Mother Teresa, Abraham Lincoln, George Washington, Winston Churchill, Eliot Ness, Paul Newman, and Nathan Hale.

What is your motto?
"Embrace good, confront evil."

March 2003

I most dislike: "The callousness with which poor people are deceived…"

What is your idea of perfect happiness?
When my consciousness, my instincts, and my values are in tune with the universe.

What is your greatest fear?
Mankind's unwitting extinction by its own misdeeds.

Which historical figure do you most identify with?
Thurgood Marshall.

Which living person do you most admire?
Nelson Mandela.

What is the trait you most deplore in yourself?
The frequent wars between my shyness and my social tendencies.

What is the trait you most deplore in others?
Impoliteness.

What is your greatest extravagance?
Books.

What is your favorite journey?
The one that started with my conception, roughly 80 years ago.

On what occasion do you lie?
First, let me disarm that loaded question. I know how easy it is for one to stay well within moral, ethical, and legal bounds through the skillful use of words—and to thereby spin, sidestep, circumvent, or bend a truth completely out of shape. To that extent, we are all liars on numerous occasions.

What do you dislike most about your appearance?
Are you trying to tell me something I don't know? Far as I can tell, I still have most of my hair, my gut is not hanging over my belt, and I still have all of my teeth.

Which living person do you most despise?
Generally, I tend to despise human behavior rather than human creatures.

What is your greatest regret?
I cannot recall what that might have been, but whatever it was, I survived it. And I have no regrets about that.

What or who is the greatest love of your life?
My wife, my six children, my five grandchildren, my one great-grandchild, and Sproutie, the family dog.

When and where were you happiest?
I was happiest making films, writing books, and surviving prostate cancer.

If you could change one thing about yourself, what would it be?
I wouldn't change a single thing, because one change alters every moment that follows it.

What do you consider your greatest achievement?
I leave that judgment to others and to history.

If you were to die and come back as a person or thing, what do you think it would be?
I don't want to come back. What for?

What is your most treasured possession?
The love of family and friends.

What is your most marked characteristic?
Discipline.

What do you most value in your friends?
Honesty.

Who are your favorite writers?
Bill Bryson, Carl Sagan, Maya Angelou, James Baldwin, Timothy Ferris, Toni Morrison, and Walter Mosley.

Who is your favorite hero of fiction?
Jason Bourne.

Who are your heroes in real life?
My mom and dad. Nelson Mandela, Barack Obama, Bill Clinton, Bill Gates, Warren Buffett, Oprah Winfrey, and Bono.

What is it that you most dislike?
The callousness with which poor people are deceived, ignored, and dismissed.

What is your motto?
"To be ever respectful of the forces of nature that designed our entrance and our exit."

February 2007

SIDNEY POITIER

ACTOR

SUMNER REDSTONE

MEDIA MOGUL

My most overused phrase: "Who are the assholes who are selling our stock?"

What is your greatest fear?
A day without a challenge or purpose—and that I won't be here tomorrow.

What is the trait you most deplore in others?
A lack of commitment.

What is your greatest extravagance?
A great meal and a nice hotel room.

What do you consider the most overrated virtue?
Patience.

Which words or phrases do you most overuse?
"Who are the assholes who are selling our stock?"

What is your greatest regret?
That my parents didn't live long enough to see the success of Viacom.

What or who is the greatest love of your life?
My family, closely followed by my work.

What do you consider your greatest achievement?
That from a few drive-in theaters I have built one of the world's largest entertainment companies.

If you were to die and come back as a person or thing, what do you think it would be?
Reincarnation is overrated. If I never leave, I won't have to come back.

What is your most treasured possession?
I don't treasure possessions. The greatest treasure is living life to the fullest.

What do you regard as the lowest depth of misery?
Viacom's stock undervalued in a bear market.

What is your most marked characteristic?
An obsessive drive to win.

What is the quality you most like in a man?
Great character, loyalty, trust—and, of course, competence.

What is the quality you most like in a woman?
The quality I like most in women is women.

What do you most value in your friends?
The willingness to tell me what I may not enjoy hearing.

Who are your favorite writers?
Just what you might expect, Dostoyevsky and Mary Higgins Clark.

Who is your favorite hero of fiction?
My favorite Rugrat, Tommy Pickles.

Who are your heroes in real life?
The doctors and nurses at Mass. General who saved my life.

What is it that you most dislike?
Waiting . . . for anything.

How would you like to die?
I would not like it at all.

What is your motto?
"Never give up; never say never; nothing is impossible."

July 2001

LOU REED

MUSICIAN

What do you consider your greatest achievement?
Walking upright.

What is your most marked characteristic?
Sensitivity, modesty, and humor.
I exist in a Leibnizian monad.

Which talent would you most like to have?
Ambidextrousness.

What do you regard as the lowest depth of misery?
Being interviewed by an English journalist.

What is your greatest fear?
Interviews in an afterlife.

What is your current state of mind?
Elated.

When and where were you happiest?
1857.

What is your idea of perfect happiness?
Rent-controlled apartment.

What is the trait you most deplore in yourself?
Too much modesty.

What is the trait you most deplore in others?
Deafness.

What is your greatest extravagance?
I have none.

What is your favorite journey?
The No. 9 train on the West Side.

What do you consider the most overrated virtue?
Frugality.

On what occasion do you lie?
Tax day.

What do you dislike most about your appearance?
Too muscular.

Which words or phrases do you most overuse?
"Chill."

What is your greatest regret?
The loss of two Harleys.

What is your most treasured possession?
My baby teeth.

What or who is the greatest love of your life?
Laurie Anderson.

What is the quality you most like in a man?
Peter Gabriel and his Witness program.

Which living person do you most admire?
Václav Havel.

Which living person do you most despise?
Rush Limbaugh, but there are so many.

If you were to die and come back as a person or thing, what do you think it would be?
An amplifier.

February 1996

My idea of perfect happiness: "Rent-controlled apartment."

My greatest achievement: "Waking up."

What is your idea of perfect happiness?
Now.

Which historical figure do you most identify with?
Me.

What is the trait you most deplore in yourself?
Modesty and humility.

What is your favorite journey?
Life.

What do you consider the most overrated virtue?
Truthfulness.

On what occasion do you lie?
When I don't know the truth.

What do you dislike most about your appearance?
When the lie doesn't work.

Which living person do you most despise?
Draw up a list.

Which words or phrases do you most overuse?
"I love you."

What is your greatest regret?
Not having one.

When and where were you happiest?
Right up to this question.

Which talent would you most like to have?
Do you mean I have to give one up?

What is your current state of mind?
Are you crazy?

If you could change one thing about yourself, what would it be?
Underwear.

If you could change one thing about your family, what would it be?
There's not enough of them.

What do you consider your greatest achievement?
Waking up.

What is your most marked characteristic?
Blinding charm.

What is the quality you most like in a woman?
Love.

What is the quality you most like in a man?
Fear.

What do you most value in your friends?
That they don't die on me.

Who is your favorite hero of fiction?
Hunter Thompson.

What is it that you most dislike?
The next question.

How would you like to die?
Later.

What is your motto?
"I told you I was sick!"

January 2003

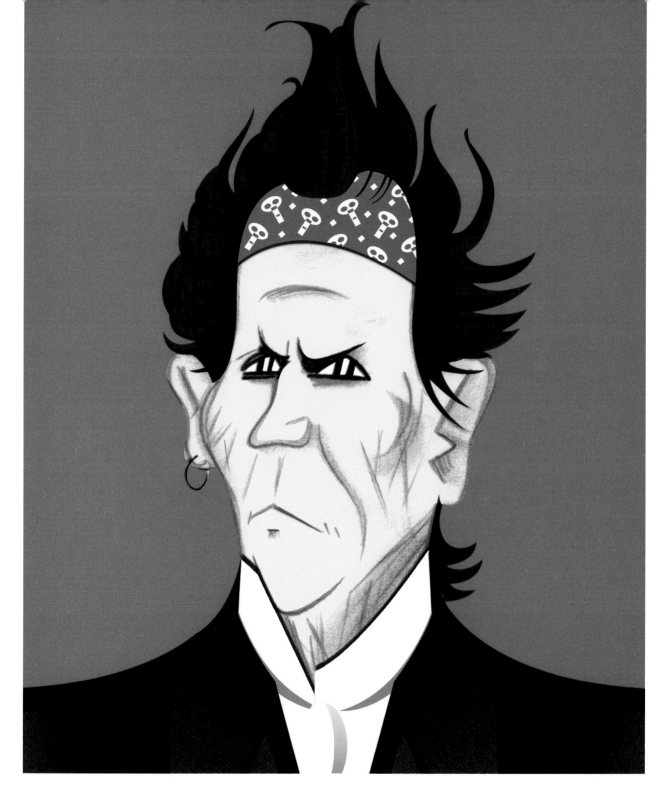

KEITH RICHARDS

MUSICIAN

JOAN RIVERS

COMEDIAN

I would like to live in: "Eighteenth-century France, but with plumbing and plastic surgery."

What is your greatest fear?
Being poor—or, worse, having Kelsey Grammer fight with Teddy Kennedy over who is to drive me home.

Which historical figure do you most identify with?
Marie Antoinette—she had great style, and her last words were "Shit, just when I got my hair right."

Which living person do you most admire?
None. Unfortunately, we are in an age of antiheroes.

What is your greatest extravagance?
Gold-leafing anything that doesn't move— and taking Marlon Brando to dinner.

What is your favorite journey?
Starting at Machu Picchu, then on to the Himalayas, and ending up in the bakery where Elvis exploded.

What do you consider the most overrated virtue?
Honesty—but I'm really lying when I say that.

On what occasion do you lie?
When it will ease a situation, avoid hurting someone I care about, or when I bump into Barbra Streisand after one of her screenings.

Which words or phrases do you most overuse?
"Relax, I'm just joking."

What is your greatest regret?
Passing on Jackie's blender at the Kennedy-estate auction.

If you could change one thing about yourself, what would it be?
I would have flesh-toned varicose veins.

If you were to die and come back as a person or thing, what do you think it would be?
Something small, like a flower… or an autumn leaf… or Jackie Chan.

What is your most treasured possession?
Besides my daughter, Melissa, and my fiancé, Orin Lehman, my bee pin from my Joan Rivers Classics Collection. It was the first item I ever sold, and it opened doors for a whole new career.

What do you regard as the lowest depth of misery?
Lack of hope… and living in L.A. without a good body.

Where would you like to live?
Eighteenth-century France, but with plumbing and plastic surgery.

What is the quality you most like in a man?
Humor, intelligence, honesty, and abs.

What is the quality you most like in a woman?
Honesty, humor, loyalty, and if she's homelier than I am, then I'm really happy.

Who are your favorite writers?
Jane Austen!!! I've seen all her movies.

Who is your favorite hero of fiction?
O. J. Simpson, from his autobiography.

What is it that you most dislike?
Raindrops on roses and whiskers on kittens… If I continue, will there be a copyright problem?

How would you like to die?
Coming offstage after a five-minute standing ovation, falling into the arms of my lover, and having the doctor look at me and say, "This is impossible! She looks much too young to go!"

What is your motto?
I have two. The first is "Get on with it." The second is "Don't eat anything you pick up off the sidewalk."

February 1997

My most overused phrase: "You dig?"

What is your idea of perfect happiness?
Perfect happiness is something which doesn't exist
in this life. The goal is to never be too happy
or never be too sad.

What is your greatest fear?
Not getting close enough to my aspirations.

Which living person do you most admire?
I'm afraid that I don't admire people that much.
Maybe my plumber.

What is the trait you most deplore in yourself?
Not always being resolute enough.

What is the trait you most deplore in others?
Slovenly personal traits.

What is your greatest extravagance?
Overindulgence in good food.

What do you consider the most overrated virtue?
Probably thriftiness.

On what occasion do you lie?
When I'm absolutely forced to by one
of life's stupid entanglements.

Which words or phrases do you most overuse?
Probably "You dig?"

What is your greatest regret?
Not saying some things to departed associates.

What or who is the greatest love of your life?
Of course my late wife, Lucille.

Which talent would you most like to have?
The one that I have.

What is your current state of mind?
Peaceful but active.

What do you consider your greatest achievement?
Listening to my inner consciousness and summoning the
strength and determination to act on it.

**If you could choose what to come back as,
what would it be?**
A more evolved, intelligent being.

What is your most treasured possession?
When I lost so many prized possessions on 9/11,
I learned a lesson: Possessions are not "where it's at."

What do you regard as the lowest depth of misery?
Being in the belly of the beast in a straitjacket.

Where would you like to live?
Wherever I can be left alone.

What is your favorite occupation?
Music, or whatever contributes to the edification of others.

What is the quality you most like in a man?
Listening more than talking.

What do you most value in your friends?
Loyalty.

Who are your heroes in real life?
Anyone whose life is lived giving more than taking.

What is your motto?
"Do unto others," and, secondly, one I made up about
watching TV: "Images and lies, and bad for your eyes."

September 2007

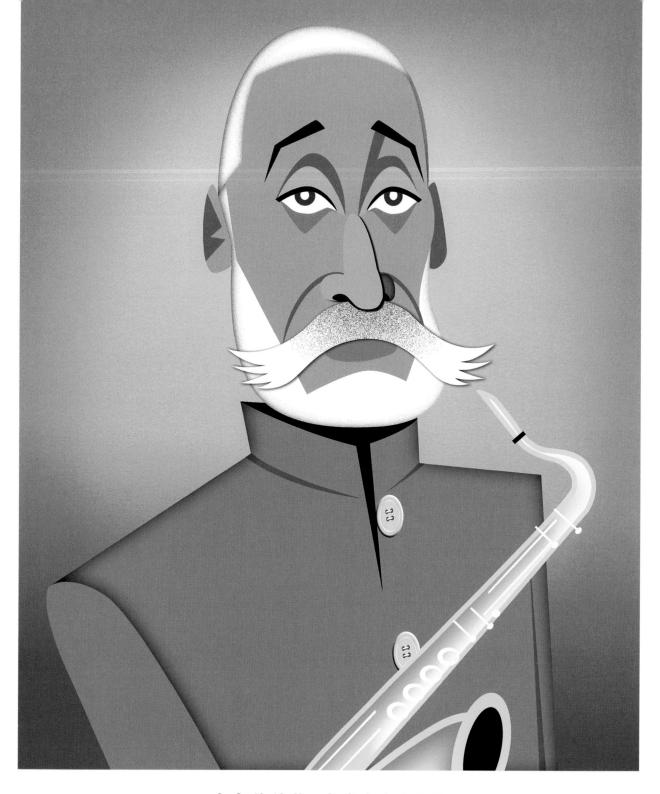

SONNY ROLLINS

JAZZ MUSICIAN

KARL ROVE

POLITICAL STRATEGIST *and* PRESIDENTIAL ADVISER

My motto: "Be prepared! Find the bastards. And pile on!"

What is your current state of mind?
Energized, challenged, ready.

What is your greatest extravagance?
Too many books.

What is your greatest fear?
Living foolishly above my means and running out of money.

What is the trait you most deplore in others?
Not being authentic.

What do you consider the most overrated virtue?
Patience.

If you could change one thing about yourself, what would it be?
Try to be more patient.

What is the quality you most like in a man?
Quiet confidence.

What is the quality you most like in a woman?
Strength of character.

Which words or phrases do you most overuse?
"Fabulous!" After that, "Look . . ." followed by an explanation.

Which talent would you most like to have?
To play a musical instrument or sing worth a darn.

What or who is the greatest love of your life?
The who are my wife and son. The what is America.

Where would you like to live?
Texas, of course.

What is your favorite occupation?
Politics.

What is your most treasured possession?
My books, starting with the first one I can ever remember reading, *Great Moments in History*.

Who are your favorite writers?
In alphabetical order: Jorge Luis Borges, Gabor Boritt, Ray Bradbury, G. K. Chesterton, Winston Churchill, David Herbert Donald, T. S. Eliot, Joseph Ellis, Gary Gallagher, F. A. Hayek, Paul Horgan, Paul Johnson, Tom Lea, C. S. Lewis, Abraham Lincoln, John D. MacDonald, David McCullough, Merrill Peterson, Robert Remini, Andrew Roberts, William Shakespeare, Adam Smith, Alexis de Tocqueville, Evelyn Waugh, and Robert Wiebe.

Who is your favorite hero of fiction?
Travis McGee or Borges himself. (Was he real? Or not?)

Who are your heroes in real life?
The men and women who volunteer to go into harm's way wearing the uniform of our country's military.

What do you most value in your friends?
Honesty and loyalty.

What is your most marked characteristic?
Energy and precision are tied.

How would you like to die?
At home in my bed asleep, sound of mind and body but just too damned old.

What is your motto?
I like the one that used to be the motto on the unit coin of the 11th Armored Cavalry Regiment, the Blackhorse: "Be prepared! Find the bastards. And pile on!"

February 2008

SALMAN RUSHDIE

WRITER

My idea of perfect happiness: "Life without policemen."

When and where were you happiest?
Now, and here.

On what occasion do you lie?
These.

What is your current state of mind?
Singing.

Which talent would you most like to have?
The ability to sing.

What is your idea of perfect happiness?
Life without policemen.

What do you consider your greatest achievement?
To have continued.

What do you consider the most overrated virtue?
Faith.

What is the trait you most deplore in yourself?
Talkativeness.

What is the trait you most deplore in others?
Silence.

What is your greatest extravagance?
Linguistic.

What is your greatest fear?
Irrelevance.

What do you dislike most about your appearance?
Its infrequency.

What is your most marked characteristic?
Droopy eyelids.

What is your greatest regret?
My second marriage.

What is your most treasured possession?
Good health.

What do you regard as the lowest depth of misery?
Any illness, however trivial.

What is the quality you most like in a man?
Warmth.

What is the quality you most like in a woman?
Humor.

Who are your favorite writers?
My friends.

Who is your favorite hero of fiction?
Leopold Bloom, Gregor Samsa, Bartleby the Scrivener.

Who are your heroes in real life?
Tennis players, film directors, rock stars.

Where would you like to live?
On bookshelves—forever.

If you were to die and come back as a person or thing, what do you think it would be?
A city street.

If you could choose what to come back as, what would it be?
A city.

How would you like to die?
I would prefer not to.

January 1996

ARNOLD SCHWARZENEGGER

ACTOR *and* CALIFORNIA GOVERNOR

The lowest depth of misery: "Did you read the reviews for *Last Action Hero*?"

What is your idea of perfect happiness?
Spending time with my family—with no phone, no fax, and no meetings.

What is your greatest fear?
I am petrified of bikini waxing. I had a very bad experience in 1978.

Which living person do you most admire?
My mother-in-law, Eunice Shriver, who founded the Special Olympics, and my father-in-law, Sargent Shriver, who founded Job Corps and was the first director of the Peace Corps.

What is the trait you most deplore in others?
People who speak with heavy American accents. I can barely understand them. No, seriously, dishonesty.

What is your greatest extravagance?
I am a major shoe queen.

What do you dislike most about your appearance?
Let's just say Milton Berle had the same exact problem. I tell you, it's a curse.

Which words or phrases do you most overuse?
"Maria, I said I'm sorry" and "Yes, dear."

What is your greatest regret?
My only regret is when an actor wins an Oscar for a role I turned down. Although I still say I wasn't right for *Forrest Gump*.

What or who is the greatest love of your life?
My wife and my four children, who have all my love and come first, above everything else.

What do you regard as the lowest depth of misery?
Did you read the reviews for *Last Action Hero*?

What do you most value in your friends?
I think I value the same things everyone does— loyalty, a sense of humor, the ability to make campaign contributions.

Who are your heroes in real life?
Teachers and principals, who are underpaid but devote their lives to making sure our kids get a good education. It's the best defense against gangs, violence, and drug use by kids—and the best chance to ensure their future.

Who are your favorite writers?
My favorite fiction writers are studio accountants.

How would you like to die?
From a heart attack at the Kodak Theatre when they announce I won best actor for *Terminator 3*.

What is your motto?
"If at first you don't succeed, try, try, try again. Then use a stunt double."

July 2003
(Schwarzenegger became governor of California in November 2003.)

MARTIN SCORSESE

FILM DIRECTOR *and* PRODUCER

What is your idea of perfect happiness?
I think you can strive to attain it, but be realistic about the outcome. In the meantime, I find I might be experiencing it through flashes or brief moments in love and art, and at times just being alive.

When and where were you happiest?
When my friends and I were making *Mean Streets,* 1973.

What is the trait you most deplore in yourself?
Laziness, wasting time. I'd like to be able to make films faster.

What is the trait you most deplore in others?
Actually, I dislike dealing with schedules and logistics—mine and others'.

What is your greatest extravagance?
Old Technicolor films—watching, collecting, or helping to restore them.

What do you consider the most overrated virtue?
Prudence.

On what occasion do you lie?
To avoid, if at all possible, a plane flight.

What do you dislike most about your appearance?
When I was acting in Tavernier's film *'Round Midnight,* I played a nightclub owner. One shot, all I had to do was walk across the room. When he said "Action" I started to walk, and I became very aware of walking. I find I'm usually walking too fast, and I don't like the way it looks. As far as the rest of me, I've learned to live with it.

If you could change one thing about yourself, what would it be?
First of all, I'd like to stop complaining—I'm beginning to annoy myself. I would like to learn to read faster, however. Again, the rest I've learned to live with.

Which words or phrases do you most overuse?
I use the word "wonderful" too much. I picked this up from cinematographer Michael Chapman. During *Taxi Driver,* checking a shot, I asked him, "Do you think that's O.K., with such and such?" He answered, "Oh, that's *wonderful,* don't touch it." And I thought the word "wonderful" was an odd way to describe a shot of the squalor of a city street. I found I enjoyed the expression "wonderful"—it's actually a wonderful word. But I've used it too much since 1975 and I'm trying to cut back.

What is your favorite journey?
Italy through to North Africa.

What is your greatest regret?
Not reading more when I was younger. Also, I admire the process of cooking, and I regret never really having had a chance to learn how to cook.

Which talent would you most like to have?
To write and play music.

What do you consider your greatest achievement?
Putting eardrops in my dog Zoë's ears. Zoë is a bichon frisé, very pretty but a little temperamental, and it usually takes two people to put in the medication. But at times I was actually able to do it alone. This was a revelation because all my life I've had asthma and allergies and could never even as much as go near animals. Then Zoë arrived and my life changed. Most of the allergies subsided—less asthma too. Above all, I learned some patience and caring in the process. To be able to deal with animals like this is something I never thought would happen in my life. However, I'm still allergic to cats.

October 1993

The most overrated virtue: "Prudence."

BOBBY SHORT

ENTERTAINER

My greatest extravagance: "Extravagance."

What is your favorite journey?
Coming home to New York City.

What is your idea of perfect happiness?
Ten consecutive hours of sleep.

What is your greatest fear?
Fear itself.

What is your most marked characteristic?
My occasional unbridled enthusiasm.

What is the trait you most deplore in yourself?
My occasional unbridled enthusiasm.

What or who is the greatest love of your life?
Music.

What do you regard as the lowest depth of misery?
Boredom.

What is your greatest extravagance?
Extravagance.

What is the trait you most deplore in others?
Envy.

Which words or phrases do you most overuse?
"Isn't it wonderful!"

What is your greatest regret?
Having been born too late to live among the people I most admire.

On what occasion do you lie?
Only when I feel there's no other way out.

When and where were you happiest?
When I was cutting my teeth in Paris.

What do you consider your greatest achievement?
Survival.

What is your most treasured possession?
My piano.

What is your favorite occupation?
Working.

What is the quality you most like in a man?
Humor.

What is the quality you most like in a woman?
Humor.

Which historical figure do you most identify with?
Duke Ellington.

How would you like to die?
In my sleep.

If you were to die and come back as a person or thing, what do you think it would be?
One ride is enough for me.

What is your motto?
"There's always tomorrow."

November 1995
(Short died in 2005.)

My favorite journey: "That weekend I gave Buddhism a shot."

What is your idea of perfect happiness?
A day without chafing.

What is your greatest fear?
Nonspecific urethritis.

Which historical figure do you most identify with?
Bess Truman.

Which living person do you most admire?
My children.

What is the trait you most deplore in yourself?
My uncontrollable urge to shoplift.

What is the trait you most deplore in others?
People who don't treat their agents like family.

What is your greatest extravagance?
Shampoo *and* conditioner.

What is your favorite journey?
That weekend I gave Buddhism a shot.

What do you consider the most overrated virtue?
Fairness.

On what occasion do you lie?
See answers below.

What do you dislike most about your appearance?
People's reaction to it.

Which talent would you most like to have?
Cure my own ham.

What is your current state of mind?
Is that with the prescription?

If you could change one thing about yourself, what would it be?
The curse of my enormous manhood.

If you could change one thing about your family, what would it be?
Living arrangements.

What do you consider your greatest achievement?
My invention of cold fusion.

If you were to die and come back as a person or thing, what do you think it would be?
A stocky male nurse.

If you could choose what to come back as, what would it be?
Male nurse with swimmer's body.

What is your most treasured possession?
My egg-crate abs.

What do you regard as the lowest depth of misery?
The premiere of *Captain Ron II.*

What is your favorite occupation?
Fluffer.

What is your most marked characteristic?
My ability to fake enthusiasm for others.

What is the quality you most like in a man?
Humor and a hairy chest.

What is the quality you most like in a woman?
See above.

What do you most value in your friends?
What they can do for my career.

What are your favorite names?
Lil and Larry.

How would you like to die?
Naked and bloated.

What is your motto?
"It's better to have loved a short than never to have loved a tall."

September 1999

MARTIN SHORT

COMEDIAN

LIZ SMITH

COLUMNIST

Perfect happiness: "Television, a thriller, a candy bar, popcorn, no telephone, all at once."

When and where were you happiest?
Now. Here in little old New York City!

What do you consider your greatest achievement?
Clinging to the lower rungs of journalism, making a living, having people yell at me in the street.

What is the trait you most deplore in others?
Lying, cheating, fudging, nudging the ethical line.

What is the trait you most deplore in yourself?
Lying, cheating, fudging, nudging the ethical line.

Which words or phrases do you most overuse?
"Great."

On what occasion do you lie?
Oh, puh-leeze!

What do you consider the most overrated virtue?
Loyalty (it gets people in a lot of absurd ethical trouble).

What is your idea of perfect happiness?
Television, a thriller, a candy bar, popcorn, no telephone, all at once.

What do you regard as the lowest depth of misery?
Public humiliation.

What is your greatest fear?
Dying a lingering painful death, becoming a pain in the ass.

What is the quality you most like in a person?
Intelligence leavened with humor.

What is it that you most dislike?
Hypocrisy.

What is your most marked characteristic?
Self-defeating generosity.

What is your greatest extravagance?
Eating in restaurants, overtipping.

Which historical figure do you most identify with?
Voltaire.

Which living person do you most despise?
They all jostle together in my head and become one big fat slobby press agent in particular.

What is your favorite journey?
The Greek islands, Greece itself.

What is your most treasured possession?
My genes from the Tiptons, McCalls, Balls, Smiths.

What do you most value in your friends?
Their infinite, unique variety.

If you were to die and come back as a person or thing, what do you think it would be?
The three monkeys—seeing, speaking, hearing no evil.

If you could choose what to come back as, what would it be?
A cat that does as it pleases.

Which talent would you most like to have?
To dance like Fred Astaire.

What is your motto?
"Dare to be true."

April 1994

"Moses proved—it's all about who you know."

What is your idea of perfect happiness?
An all-Yiddish-speaking Canada.

Which historical figure do you most identify with?
Moses, who proved that it's all about who you know.

What is the trait you most deplore in yourself?
Let me see. I'm thinking. Can I get back to you on this?
O.K., procrastination.

What is the trait you most deplore in others?
Outing a C.I.A. agent because you're
pissed about something else.

What is your greatest extravagance?
My dog, Izzy. A big poodle so smart he's now learning
how to punch up my scripts.

What is your favorite journey?
The journey from the Manitoba tundra
to subbing for Johnny Carson.

What do you consider the most overrated virtue?
Taking over a country and forcing democracy on it.

On what occasion do you lie?
Mostly after I've seen anyone perform.

What do you dislike most about your appearance?
Maintaining it.

Which living person do you most despise?
I don't despise people, but a lot of them
sure annoy the hell out of me.

What is your greatest regret?
When I stood short and did it their way.

What or who is the greatest love of your life?
Obviously my lovely wife, who's bound to read this.

When and where were you happiest?
During Watergate, when I was comparing
Nixon's face to a foot.

**If you could change one thing about yourself,
what would it be?**
Less raw sensuality.

Which words or phrases do you most overuse?
"He's a big dog, but he's very friendly."

What is your greatest fear?
Pork.

What do you consider your greatest achievement?
Being on Nixon's enemies list.

**If you could choose what to come back as,
what would it be?**
Frank Sinatra's dick—the early years.

What is your most treasured possession?
The memory of my brother.

What do you regard as the lowest depth of misery?
My daughters' dating during their teenage years.

Where would you like to live?
In infamy. Barring that, Malibu.

What is your favorite occupation?
Mine. Hanging out with friends whose job is to make
people laugh. What could be better?

What is your most marked characteristic?
There is no level of incompetence that I can't identify with.

What is the quality you most like in a man?
I like a man who can come to my house and fix things.

What is the quality you most like in a woman?
The same as above.

What do you most value in your friends?
They're funny. Funny matters.

Who are your favorite writers?
Mark Twain. Philip Roth. Paddy Chayefsky.

Who is your favorite hero of fiction?
Tonto. Imagine how hard it is to be the friend
of the Lone Ranger.

How would you like to die?
Quickly, after getting a laugh.

What is your motto?
"When the owl screams, the hunter pisses on his boot."

June 2007

DAVID STEINBERG

COMEDIAN *and* FILMMAKER

HOWARD STERN

COMEDIAN, COMMENTATOR, *and* TALK-SHOW HOST

"I guess I'm a sensitive guy deep down."

What or who is the greatest love of your life?
Me. I love everything about me.
Everyone else has faults.

What is your greatest achievement?
A No. 1 radio show across the entire country,
two best-sellers, the highest-grossing pay-per-view
entertainment special in history, and successfully
corrupting the morals of an entire generation.

What is your idea of perfect happiness?
A stranger putting her hands down my pants.

What is your greatest fear?
I'm at a radio convention surrounded by idiots
like the bloated Rush Limbaugh and he eats so much
his giant pumpkin head explodes all over me.

What is it that you most dislike?
Anytime anyone besides me is successful.

Which words or phrases do you most overuse?
"Dude" and "Kiss my ass in Macy's window,
you stupid rat Jap bastard."

When and where were you happiest?
Summer camp surrounded by Jews.

What is your current state of mind?
I am sad. I am always sad.

What is the trait you most deplore in others?
Stupidity. There are people out there who take life way too
seriously because they are too dumb to get the joke.

Which living person do you most despise?
There would be 12 of them. The idiots who sat on O.J.'s jury.

What is your greatest extravagance?
My bathroom. It's white marble and it's way too big.

What is your favorite journey?
I hate all journeys. My biggest fear is leaving
the house, and I'd prefer that my greatest journey
be to the kitchen and back.

**If you could change one thing about yourself,
what would it be?**
The fear that I make my living in radio. I think circus
clowns have more prestige.

What is your favorite occupation?
Social worker. I have a strong desire to help fucked-up
slobs with no hope in their lives whatsoever. I don't
know—I guess I'm a sensitive guy deep down.

What is your most marked characteristic?
My pretty feet. They look good with a little polish and
wrapped in my fine leather sandals.

What is the quality you most like in a man?
I like eyes, broad shoulders, and hands.

What is the quality you most like in a woman?
Eyes, broad shoulders, and hands.

What do you most value in your friends?
The ability to keep their mouths shut.

Who are your favorite writers?
The entire staff of *The National Enquirer*.
They write simply and elegantly.

**If you were to die and come back as a person or thing,
what do you think it would be?**
God would most likely want to punish me,
so I'd come back as Larry King's first wife.

How would you like to die?
At the hands of Fidel Castro while invading Cuba.

What is your greatest regret?
Doing this interview.

March 1997

STING

MUSICIAN

The trait I most deplore in myself: "Equivocation." In others: "Blind certainty."

What is your idea of perfect happiness?
Singing my head off.

What is your greatest fear?
Fear itself.

Which historical figure do you most identify with?
Captain Bligh.

Which living person do you most admire?
Nelson Mandela.

What is the trait you most deplore in yourself?
Equivocation.

What is the trait you most deplore in others?
Blind certainty.

What is your greatest extravagance?
My home.

What is your favorite journey?
Going home.

What do you consider the most overrated virtue?
Blind faith.

On what occasion do you lie?
Only when absolutely necessary.

What do you dislike most about your appearance?
Its ubiquity.

What is your greatest regret?
Je ne regrette rien!

What or who is the greatest love of your life?
My wife.

When and where were you happiest?
Here, right now.

What is your current state of mind?
Curious.

What do you consider your greatest achievement?
My family.

What is your most treasured possession?
My mental and physical health.

What is the quality you most like in a man?
Honesty.

What is the quality you most like in a woman?
Intelligence.

What is the quality you most value in your friends?
Honesty, intelligence, and humor.

Who is your favorite hero of fiction?
Huckleberry Finn.

What is your motto?
"Die without fear."

July 2000

How I would like to die:
"By the river, in Scotland, clutching a good bottle of wine."

What is your idea of perfect happiness?
Hot weather in Scotland.

What is your current state of mind?
Overstimulated.

What is your greatest fear?
Losing a child. Knives.

What is the trait you most deplore in yourself?
Greed.

What is the trait you most deplore in others?
Greed.

What is your greatest extravagance?
Wine.

What do you consider the most overrated virtue?
Cleanliness.

What is it that you most dislike?
Bigotry.

On what occasion do you lie?
To get out of going to things.

What do you dislike most about your appearance?
Dimply thighs.

What is the quality you most like in a man?
Uxoriousness.

What is the quality you most like in a woman?
Ability to laugh in the face of disaster.

Which words or phrases do you most overuse?
"I have to say... ", "Is it time for a drink?"

What or who is the greatest love of your life?
My family.

When and where were you happiest?
Just after giving birth without painkillers.

Which talent would you most like to have?
To play the piano exceptionally well.

If you could change one thing about yourself, what would it be?
Then who would I be?

If you were to die and come back as a person or thing, what do you think it would be?
A human being. Again.

What is your most treasured possession?
My Finnish sauna.

What do you regard as the lowest depth of misery?
Clinical depression. Exile.

What is your most marked characteristic?
Enthusiasm. Lots of teeth.

What do you most value in your friends?
Humor.

Who are your favorite writers?
Carver, George Eliot, Austen, Twain, Spike Milligan.

Who is your favorite hero of fiction?
Sherlock Holmes.

Which historical figure do you most identify with?
[British socialist and early feminist] Annie Besant.

Who are your heroes in real life?
[Ugandan AIDS activist] Noerine Kaleeba and [British human-rights activist] Helen Bamber. My father, Eric Thompson. My husband, Greg Wise.

What are your favorite names?
Gaia, Tindy, Ernie, and Walter.

What is your greatest regret?
Not having been able to have more children.

How would you like to die?
By the river, in Scotland, clutching a good bottle of wine.

July 2008

EMMA THOMPSON

ACTRESS

DONALD TRUMP
REAL-ESTATE DEVELOPER

What is your idea of perfect happiness?
Good health and being with a great person.

Which historical figure do you most identify with?
Considering his work and love for
New York City, I would say Robert Moses.

Which living person do you most admire?
I don't admire living people, I respect them.

What is your greatest extravagance?
Having to only ride an elevator to get to work.

What is your favorite journey?
From Trump Tower to Mar-a-Lago, in Palm Beach.

What do you dislike most about your appearance?
That I look different than I did when I was 33.

Which living person do you most despise?
I despise many living people.

Which words or phrases do you most overuse?
None of them. When I say something is great
or the best, to me that's not overuse, it's the truth.
But perhaps "You're fired!"

What is your greatest regret?
The loss of my brother Fred.

What or who is the greatest love of your life?
My family, which now includes Melania.

Which talent would you most like to have?
To be able to play golf like Tiger Woods,
Phil Mickelson, or Ernie Els.

**If you could change one thing about yourself,
what would it be?**
My hair!

**If you could change one thing about your family,
what would it be?**
It'd be nice if my parents were still around
to see what has happened with me.

**If you were to die and come back as a person or thing,
what do you think it would be?**
A great building in New York City.

What is the quality you most like in a man?
Integrity and loyalty—although they
are almost the same thing, at least to me.

What is the quality you most like in a woman?
Great beauty, both inside and out.

Who are your favorite writers?
There are so many great ones, I can't mention them all.
But one of the best is one of the biggest sellers—myself.

Who is your favorite hero of fiction?
James Bond.

Who are your heroes in real life?
Abraham Lincoln, Winston Churchill, Ronald Reagan.

What are your favorite names?
Melania, Don, Ivanka, Eric, and Tiffany.

How would you like to die?
Happily in bed.

What is your motto?
"Think big—and get the job done!"

September 2004

If I could come back as a person or thing, it would be as: "A great building in New York City."

LIV ULLMANN

ACTRESS

My idea of perfect happiness: "To recognize and be recognized."

What is your idea of perfect happiness?
To recognize and be recognized.

What is your current state of mind?
Peaceful.

What is the trait you most deplore in yourself?
My urge to please.

On what occasion do you lie?
When I try to please.

What is your greatest extravagance?
Phoning and travel.

What is your favorite journey?
A spiritual one. Or through a great book—or through a great composer or through a great film or theater experience.

What do you dislike most about your appearance?
I like my appearance—and have curiosity over the astonishing changes I have gone and shall go through.

Which living person do you most despise?
Talking heads on TV when they throw stones from their own crooked glass houses.

Which words or phrases do you most overuse?
"Yes."

What is your greatest regret?
Sometimes I said "Yes."

When and where were you happiest?
The 24 hours when I gave birth and looked at her in my arms and knew that life was a miracle.

What do you consider your greatest achievement?
That I look forward to the day—as when I was young.

Where would you like to live?
Like I do—in different countries, but having roots in one.

What is your favorite occupation?
Creating.

What do you most value in your friends?
That they like to laugh. That they feel for others and that they have wisdom to share.

Who are your favorite writers?
Hamsun, Proust, Hugo, Tolstoy, and all the good poets of our world—and so many more writers who have changed my life.

Who is your favorite hero of fiction?
I liked Alice who wandered through the mirror, and all the animals in Winnie-the-Pooh.

How would you like to die?
Serene and with curiosity over "How will it be now?"

What is your motto?
"For whom the bell tolls—it tolls for me."

February 1999

My greatest fear:
"Elevation to the papacy."

What is your idea of perfect happiness?
Filling out questionnaires.

What is your greatest fear?
Elevation to the papacy.

Which historical figure do you most identify with?
Thomas Paine.

Which living person do you most admire?
Jesse Jackson.

What is the trait you most deplore in yourself?
A sense of justice.

What is the trait you most deplore in others?
Ignorance.

What is your favorite journey?
To bed.

What do you consider the most overrated virtue?
Patriotism.

On what occasion do you lie?
To convey truth to others.

What do you dislike most about your appearance?
White hair turning blond after being dyed for a film.

Which living person do you most despise?
William Safire.

What is your greatest regret?
My presidency.

What or who is the greatest love of your life?
Bombay gin.

When and where were you happiest?
Drinking the above.

Which talent would you most like to have?
To write like Mozart—Salieri will do.

What is your current state of mind?
Amused at century's end.

If you could change one thing about yourself, what would it be?
Optimism.

If you could change one thing about your family, what would it be?
Them.

What do you consider your greatest achievement?
Duluth.

If you were to die and come back as a person or thing, what do you think it would be?
Nothing.

If you could choose what to come back as, what would it be?
An eternal amoeba.

What is your most treasured possession?
My timing.

What do you regard as the lowest depth of misery?
A mirror.

What is your favorite occupation?
Making sentences.

What is your most marked characteristic?
Serenity.

What is the quality you most like in a man?
Womanliness.

What is the quality you most like in a woman?
Manliness.

Who are your favorite writers?
Montaigne, Petronius, L. Frank Baum.

Who is your favorite hero of fiction?
Vautrin.

Who are your heroes in real life?
Dr. Kevorkian.

What are your favorite names?
Bill, Hillary, Chelsea.

What is it that you most dislike?
Press media. Bio-porn.

What is your motto?
"From the One, Many."

October 1994

GORE VIDAL

WRITER

DIANE VON FURSTENBERG

FASHION DESIGNER

"You only regret things you don't do… I try to do it all."

What is your idea of perfect happiness?
Hiking in the woods.

Which living person do you most admire?
The Dalai Lama.

What is the trait you most deplore in yourself?
Too impulsive.

What is your greatest extravagance?
Daily private yoga classes and weekly facials at Tracie Martyn.

On what occasion do you lie?
Never.

What do you dislike most about your appearance?
I have no waist.

Which words or phrases do you most overuse?
"Do you love me?"

What is your greatest regret?
You only regret things you don't do … I try to do it all.

What or who is the greatest love of your life?
My children and my husband.

Which talent would you most like to have?
To write well.

If you could change one thing about yourself, what would it be?
I would like to have a longer neck.

If you could change one thing about your family, what would it be?
Nothing.

What do you consider your greatest achievement?
That I appreciate life every day.

If you were to die and come back as a person or thing, what do you think it would be?
A man.

If you could choose what to come back as, what would it be?
A powerful, beautiful tree in the middle of a village square in Italy.

What is the quality you most like in a man?
Shyness combined with intelligence.

What is the quality you most like in a woman?
Strength.

What do you most value in your friends?
Loyalty.

Who are your favorite writers?
Manuel Puig, Günter Grass, Thomas Mann, and Gabriel García Márquez.

Who is your favorite hero of fiction?
Don Quixote.

Who are your heroes in real life?
My mother.

What are your favorite names?
Alexandre and Tatiana.

What is your motto?
"Go for it."

September 2003

The quality I most value in my friends: "Jumper cables and a tow chain."

What is your idea of perfect happiness?
Happiness is never perfect.

What is your greatest fear?
Being buried alive.

Which historical figure do you most identify with?
Cantinflas.

What is your favorite journey?
Actually, I don't own any of their records.

What do you consider the most overrated virtue?
Honesty.

On what occasion do you lie?
Who needs an occasion?

Which words or phrases do you most overuse?
"Do as I say and no one will get hurt."

What or who is the greatest love of your life?
My wife, Kathleen.

When and where were you happiest?
Nineteen sixty-three, one A.M., washing dishes on a Saturday night in the kitchen of Napoleone Pizza House, 619 National Avenue, National City, California.

Which talent would you most like to have?
Being able to fix the truck.

If you could choose what to come back as, what would it be?
A bull in Wyoming.

What do you regard as the lowest depth of misery?
The floor just below that.

Where would you like to live?
Hotel Esmarelda, Storyville.

What is your favorite occupation?
Blacksmith, ventriloquist, magician, jockey, train conductor, tree surgeon, and lion tamer.

What is your most marked characteristic?
My ability to discuss, in depth, a book I've never read.

What is the quality you most like in a man?
Generosity, irony, bravery, humor, madness, imagination, and the ability to take a punch.

What is the quality you most like in a woman?
Good bones, sharp teeth, big heart, black humor, full of magic, plenty of forgiveness, and a good sport.

What do you most value in your friends?
Jumper cables and a tow chain.

Who are your favorite writers?
Rod Serling, Breece D'J Pancake, Charles Bukowski, Woody Guthrie, Bill Hicks, Fellini, Frank Stanford, Willie Dixon, Bob Dylan, O. Henry.

Who is your favorite hero of fiction?
Frankenstein. And Dumbo.

How would you like to die?
I don't think I would like it very much at all.

November 2004

TOM WAITS

MUSICIAN

MIKE WALLACE

BROADCAST JOURNALIST

The trait I most deplore in myself: "Self-absorption." In others: "Self-absorption."

What is your idea of perfect happiness?
There's no such thing.

What is your greatest fear?
I don't have any left. I've already lost a son. I guess, maybe, that my wife would leave me, but she wouldn't dare.

Which historical figure do you most identify with?
Diogenes.

What is the trait you most deplore in yourself?
Self-absorption.

What is the trait you most deplore in others?
Self-absorption.

What is your greatest extravagance?
I don't have one. I'm too frugal—ask my wife.

What is your favorite journey?
To work, wherever.

What do you dislike most about your appearance?
My skinny bowlegs.

Which living person do you most despise?
Hey, I'm bipartisan.

What is your greatest regret?
Not enough time with my kids through the years.

When and where were you happiest?
Nineteen thirty-nine. Grand Rapids, Michigan. Station WOOD, 20 bucks a week.

What is your current state of mind?
Bewildered. Where are we and where is the world?

If you could change one thing about yourself, what would it be?
Suffocate my candor.

What do you consider your greatest achievement?
Still hangin' at 87.

What is your most treasured possession?
Home on the Vineyard.

What do you regard as the lowest depth of misery?
Suicidal memories of depression.

Where would you like to live?
Right here in God's country, New York City.

What is your most marked characteristic?
Marks from a bad case of acne. I was always happy when it was a gray rather than a sunshiny day.

What is the quality you most like in a man?
Loyalty.

What is the quality you most like in a woman?
Honesty.

Who are your favorite writers?
Andy Rooney.

Who are your heroes in real life?
Martin Luther King Jr. He is the man. When Lyndon Johnson was doing everything he could to make black folks happier, King had the balls to come out against participation in Vietnam, taking on his greatest supporter.

What is your motto?
From my high-school yearbook, "Hold the fort, I'm coming." Now? "Fuck 'em."

November 2005

BARBARA WALTERS

BROADCAST JOURNALIST

Perfect happiness: "A fireplace, a book, and a snowy day, with no possibility of getting in to the office."

What is your idea of perfect happiness?
A fireplace, a book, and a snowy day, with no possibility of getting in to the office.

What is your greatest fear?
Heights.

Whom do you most admire?
Christopher and Dana Reeve. Robert and Michelle Smithdas—teachers who are both deaf and blind. Oprah Winfrey.

What is your favorite journey?
To my home.

What do you consider the most overrated virtue?
Silence.

On what occasion do you lie?
To spare feelings, or cancel cocktail parties.

What do you dislike most about your appearance?
How much time do you have?

Which words or phrases do you most overuse?
"To make a long story short . . . "

What is your greatest regret?
Not keeping a diary.

What or who is the greatest love of your life?
My daughter, Jackie.

When and where were you happiest?
In Paris and Italy, the summer after graduating from college.

Which talent would you most like to have?
To sing, play the piano, and to drive.

If you could change one thing about your family, what would it be?
That they would still be here.

If you were to die and come back as a person or thing, what do you think it would be?
Me. And do it all over again with more vacations.

What is your most treasured possession?
My friends.

What do you regard as the lowest depth of misery?
Losing a child.

What is your favorite occupation?
It sure wouldn't be cooking.

What is your most marked characteristic?
My drive.

What is the quality you most like in a man?
A sense of humor and a private plane.

What is the quality you most like in a woman?
A sense of humor and a private plane.

Who are your favorite writers?
Edith Wharton and C. P. Snow.

Who is your favorite hero of fiction?
The Little Prince.

Who are your heroes in real life?
Anyone who works with the disabled.

What is it that you most dislike?
Calamari.

How would you like to die?
In my sleep, in the year 2050.

What is your motto?
"This too shall pass."

October 2004

What is your idea of perfect happiness?
A large box of Jujyfruits.

What do you consider your greatest achievement?
Making trash 1 percent more respectable.

What is your most marked characteristic?
Pencil-thin mustache.

What is your most treasured possession?
My library.

Which historical figure do you most identify with?
Saint Catherine of Siena.

What is your favorite journey?
Home to Baltimore.

What do you consider the most overrated virtue?
Rabid patriotism.

What do you dislike most about your appearance?
I've had a bad-hair life.

Which living person do you most despise?
All snitches.

Which words or phrases do you most overuse?
"You know what I mean?"

What is your greatest regret?
Nicotine.

What or who is the greatest love of your life?
I doubt that person would want to be named in *Vanity Fair*.

When and where were you happiest?
Now in both Manhattan and Baltimore.

If you could change one thing about your family, what would it be?
At last, we don't try to change one another.

What do you regard as the lowest depth of misery?
Sports.

What is it that you most dislike?
Male anti-abortion zealots.

What is your favorite occupation?
Criminal-defense lawyer for the damned.

Who are your heroes in real life?
Cy Twombly, Martin Scorsese, Glenn Gould.

What are your favorite names?
Johnny Spain, Lord Haw-Haw, Carlos the Jackal.

How would you like to die?
In my sleep after finishing the last page of a new script.

If you were to die and come back as a person or thing, what do you think it would be?
Coming back from death as somebody else is scarier than Christian hell.

If you could choose what to come back as, what would it be?
A mirror in a Douglas Sirk film.

What is your motto?
"'Each to their own,' said the old lady as she kissed the cow."

September 1998

My greatest achievement: "Making trash 1 percent more respectable."

JOHN WATERS

WRITER *and* FILMMAKER

ANDREW WEIL

PHYSICIAN, AUTHOR, *and* HEALTH ADVOCATE

My idea of perfect happiness: "Having no desires."

What do you consider your greatest achievement?
Achieving success without compromising my values.

What is your idea of perfect happiness?
Having no desires.

What is your current state of mind?
I'm feeling rather New Yorkish.

What is your most treasured possession?
My intuition.

What or who is the greatest love of your life?
Discovery.

What is your favorite journey?
The one that leads to self-discovery.

What is it that you most dislike?
A closed mind.

What is your greatest fear?
Not being equal to the demands life makes on me.

What is your greatest extravagance?
Buying plants, flowers, and bulbs.

Which living person do you most despise?
It's a waste of time and energy to despise.

What is your greatest regret?
At the moment, having agreed to answer all these questions.

Which talent would you most like to have?
Athletic grace, like that of a champion gymnast.

Where would you like to live?
Right where I do live—in the mountains outside Tucson, Arizona.

What is the trait you most deplore in yourself?
Laziness.

What is the trait you most deplore in others?
Talking too much, especially when accompanied by an inability to listen.

What do you most value in your friends?
Acceptance of me as I am, with all of my eccentricities and imperfections.

Who is your favorite hero of fiction?
Captain Marvel (the old, "Shazam!" one).

Who are your heroes in real life?
The Buddha.

Which living person do you most admire?
C. Everett Koop, M.D.

What are your favorite names?
I've always liked Andrew—it comes from the Greek word for "manly."

How would you like to die?
Consciously.

If you were to die and come back as a person or thing, what do you think it would be?
A tree.

If you could choose what to come back as, what would it be?
A giant sequoia.

What is your motto?
"Never take no for an answer."

December 1997

My motto: "Be cool."

What is your greatest fear?
Dying.

Which historical figure do you most identify with?
Thomas Edison, because he turned on the lights.

Which living person do you most admire?
Phil Spector.

What is the trait you most deplore in yourself?
Being deaf in my right ear.

What is your greatest extravagance?
Food.

On what occasion do you lie?
I don't lie.

What do you dislike most about your appearance?
My face.

Which living person do you most despise?
I don't think I should say.
I would hate for it to get back to them.

What is your greatest regret?
To have taken LSD. It was a far-out trip.
I took it twice and I didn't like it.

What or who is the greatest love of your life?
My wife, Melinda.

Which talent would you most like to have?
I wish I could talk better, in conversation.
I'm not a good talker.

If you could change one thing about yourself, what would it be?
I would like to talk with a deeper, more masculine voice.

If you could change one thing about your family, what would it be?
I would call Wendy more often.

If you could choose what to come back as, what would it be?
I would come back as a movie star.

What is your most treasured possession?
My wife.

What do you regard as the lowest depth of misery?
Losing my brothers.

Where would you like to live?
Santa Barbara.

What is the quality you most like in a man?
The ability to talk cool shit.

What is the quality you most like in a woman?
Legs.

What is it that you most dislike?
Feeling scared.

How would you like to die?
In my sleep.

What is your motto?
"Be cool."

August 2001

BRIAN WILSON

MUSICIAN *and* COMPOSER

On the pages that follow, we invite you to fill out
your own Proust Questionnaire . . .
quill pens preferred.

What is your idea of perfect happiness?_____

What is your greatest fear?_____

Which historical figure do you most identify with?_____

Which living person do you most admire?_____

What is the trait you most deplore in yourself?_____

What is the trait you most deplore in others?_____

What is your greatest extravagance?_____

What is your favorite journey?_____

What do you consider the most overrated virtue?_____

On what occasion do you lie?_____

What do you dislike most about your appearance?_____

Which living person do you most despise?_____

Which words or phrases do you most overuse?

What is your greatest regret?

What or who is the greatest love of your life?

When and where were you happiest?

Which talent would you most like to have?

What is your current state of mind?

If you could change one thing about yourself, what would it be?

If you could change one thing about your family, what would it be?

What do you consider your greatest achievement?

If you were to die and come back as a person or thing, what do you think it would be?

If you could choose what to come back as, what would it be?

What is your most treasured possession?

What do you regard as the lowest depth of misery?

Where would you like to live?

What is your favorite occupation?

What is your most marked characteristic?

What is the quality you most like in a man?

What is the quality you most like in a woman?

What do you most value in your friends?

Who are your favorite writers?

Who is your favorite hero of fiction?

Who are your heroes in real life?

What are your favorite names?

What is it that you most dislike?

How would you like to die?

What is your motto?

✦ ACKNOWLEDGMENTS ✦

EDITOR

Graydon Carter

V.F. BOOKS EDITOR

David Friend

MANAGING EDITOR

Chris Garrett

DESIGN DIRECTOR

David Harris

PROUST-COLUMN EDITORS

Aimée Bell

Carolyn Bielfeldt

Dana Brown

Riza Cruz

Jonathan Kelly

PRODUCTION DIRECTOR

Martha Hurley

SENIOR DESIGNER

Piper Vitale

ART PRODUCTION

Beth Bartholomew

EDITORIAL ASSISTANT

Feifei Sun

ILLUSTRATOR

Risko

Special thanks go to Rodale's team, led by Colin Dickerman and Chris Krogermeier and including Nancy Bailey, Chris Rhoads, Gayle Diehl, Brent Gallenberger, Caroline McCall, Brooke Myers, and Gena Smith.

We extend our gratitude as well to *Vanity Fair's* Dori Amarito, Dina Amarito-DeShan, John Banta, Peter Devine, David Foxley, Anne Fulenwider, SunHee C. Grinnell, Heather Halberstadt, Bruce Handy, Michael Hogan, Claire Howorth, Punch Hutton, Ellen Kiell, Beth Kseniak, Wayne Lawson, Anjali Lewis, Sara Marks, Amanda Meigher, Edward J. Menicheschi, Cullen Murphy, Brenda Oliveri, Elise O'Shaughnessy, Henry Porter, Jeannie Rhodes, Michael Roberts, Jane Sarkin, Krista Smith, Doug Stumpf, Robert Walsh, Julie Weiss, and Susan White, along with everyone on the magazine's art, copy, research, special-projects, photography, production, public-relations, and Web staffs.

For *Vanity Fair* production work beyond the call of duty, many thanks to Peggy Bates, Laura Bell, Valerie Bitici, Kate Brindisi, Marsha Cottrell, Pat Craven, Chris George, Sumana Ghosh, Leslie Hertzog, Michael Hipwell, H. Scott Jolley, Joel Katz, Theresa Lee, Timothy Mislock, Susan Rasco, Nancy Sampson, Anderson Tepper, and Julia Wachtel.

In the incomparable copy department: David Fenner, Adam Nadler, John Branch, James Cholakis, Scott Ferguson, Florence Fletcher, Diane Hodges, Mary Lyn Maiscott, Sophie Miodownik, Robert Morrow, S. P. Nix, and Sylvia Topp.

And for their peerless reporting and research talents: Judy DeYoung, Laura Griffin, and Helen Vera.

We are also grateful to our friends and colleagues at Sabin, Bermant & Gould; the Wylie Agency; and the Rights and Permissions Department of Condé Nast Publications.

✦ ✦ ✦

Graydon Carter has been the editor of
Vanity Fair since 1992. He edited *Vanity Fair's
Hollywood* (Viking Studio, 2000), *Oscar Night* (Knopf, 2004),
Vanity Fair: The Portraits (Abrams, 2008), and *Vanity Fair's Tales
of Hollywood* (Penguin, 2008), and wrote *What We've Lost:
How the Bush Administration Has Curtailed Our Freedoms,
Mortgaged Our Economy, Ravaged Our Environment, and Damaged Our
Standing in the World* (Farrar, Straus and Giroux, 2004).
Carter served as a producer of the films *The Kid Stays in the Picture,
Chicago 10, Surfwise,* and *Gonzo,* and won Emmy and
Peabody Awards for his work as executive producer of the CBS
documentary *9/11,* which aired in 140 countries.
A former writer at *Time* and *Life,* Carter co-founded *Spy* magazine
and served as the editor of *The New York Observer.*
He is also an owner of the New York City restaurants
the Waverly Inn, in Greenwich Village,
and the Monkey Bar, on East 54th Street.

Robert Risko is one of the most renowned celebrity
caricaturists working today. Since 1978, when Andy Warhol gave
him his first assignment for *Interview* magazine, Risko has drawn
portraits of hundreds of notables from the worlds of film and
television, music and art, politics and literature. In addition to
countless images for *Vanity Fair, Rolling Stone, The New Yorker,* and
other major magazines, Risko, author of *The Risko Book,* has
illustrated book jackets, video covers, movie posters,
and CD packages. He lives in New York City.

✦ ✦ ✦